SEMINAR STUDIES IN HISTORY

Editor: Patrick Richardson

The Rise of British Trade Unions 1825-1914

Harry Browne

LONGMAN

LONGMAN GROUP LIMITED
*Longman House, Burnt Mill, Harlow, Essex CM20 2JE, England
and Associated Companies throughout the World.*

First published 1979
Third impression 1984
ISBN 0 582 35230 4

Set in 10/11 Press Roman IBM

*Printed in Hong Kong by
Wilture Printing Co. Ltd.*

I should like to acknowledge my debt to my colleague, Michael Murphy, at CCAT who gave so generously of his time in discussing earlier drafts of this book and to Patrick Richardson, the general editor of the series, for his close, careful and helpful scrutiny of the manuscript.

For permission to use the photograph on the cover, we are grateful to the Trades Union Congress, London.

Contents

Abbreviations

ASCJ	Amalgamated Society of Carpenters and Joiners
ASE	Amalgamated Society of Engineers
ASLEF	Associated Society of Locomotive Engineers and Firemen
ASRS	Amalgamated Society of Railway Servants
GNCTU	Grand National Consolidated Trades Union
ILP	Independent Labour Party
JSEMMFS	Journeymen Steam Engine and Machine Makers Friendly Society
LRC	Labour Representation Committee
LTC	London Trades Council
NUR	National Union of Railwaymen
MFGB	Miners Federation of Great Britain
NAPL	National Association for the Protection of Labour
NTWF	National Transport Workers Federation
SDF	Social Democratic Federation
TUC	Trades Union Congress

Introduction to the Series

The seminar method of teaching is being used increasingly. It is a way of learning in smaller groups through discussion, designed both to get away from and to supplement the basic lecture techniques. To be successful, the members of a seminar must be informed – or else, in the unkind phrase of a cynic – it can be a 'pooling of ignorance'. The chapter in the textbook of English or European history by its nature cannot provide material in this depth, but at the same time the full academic work may be too long and perhaps too advanced.

For this reason we have invited practising teachers to contribute short studies on specialised aspects of British and European history with these special needs in mind. For this series the authors have been asked to provide, in addition to their basic analysis, a full selection of documentary material of all kinds and an up-to-date and comprehensive bibliography. Both these sections are referred to in the text, but it is hoped that they will prove to be valuable teaching and learning aids in themselves.

Note on the System of References:
A bold number in round brackets (**5**) in the text refers the reader to the corresponding entry in the Bibliography section at the end of the book.

A bold number in square brackets, preceded by 'doc' [**docs 6,8**] refers the reader to the corresponding items in the section of Documents, which follows the main text.

PATRICK RICHARDSON
General Editor

PART ONE

The Background

1 Introduction

In this late stage of capitalism the trade union in Britain has become a source of advice, a means of negotiation, a spokesman in dealing with employers, an adviser to governments. Functions it once had, in particular those of providing a minimal social security, have been taken over by the state itself. The trade union is institutionalised, a recognised part of the protective devices which operate in modern society to further the interests of its members where other and more traditional forms of protection have long since disappeared or have become irrelevant. At best the trade union represents a community of interests to which a worker belongs, a community which shields him within the larger society of industry and represents his interests to the state and to the government of the day.

Trade unions have come to be feared in some quarters as a brute economic force, standing for the organised power of the working class, with only a minimal concern for the overall performance of the economy or even the profitability of their own section of British industry. A different and more conciliatory view sees the trade unions, like employers' federations, as having much at stake in the development of the economy, as advising their members on restraint in pay demands and acting, at times, as unacknowledged partners to government itself in the creation of policies which will reduce inflation. During the 'voluntary' pay policy initiated by the Labour Government in the mid 1970s such a role was consistently maintained by British trade unions. The only analogy, not indeed very close, discussed in this book, is the cooperation between employers and trade unions involved in the working of the sliding scale, or in conciliation boards; but for most of the period which this book covers, the heroic age of trade unionism, their basic, necessary, concern was not 'the state of trade'. It was the interests of their members in the bread-and-butter matters of wages, conditions, welfare benefits, in what Sidney and Beatrice Webb in their classical study of trade union history (25) call 'the Standard of Life'. This concern could be seen as defensive, protective of standards already achieved, as in the 1910s, or as an advancing standard to be sought by legislation on shorter hours, greater safety at work, minimum wages as well as by collective bargaining within the industry. In the late nineteenth century, trade unionists working with the Liberals to

3

improve the statutory basis of the standard of life thought of collective bargaining as another means to achieve the same end.

To bring the trade unions into a more positive role in economic development blunts the militancy which has sporadically marked their history and forces on their members the need to think in terms more general than is traditional. At one time Owenite trade unionism seemed to offer the prospect of an alternative economic organisation, as did late nineteenth century socialism or pre-1914 syndicalism. Their present role is largely concerned not with offering alternative models in economic organisation but with working within a capitalist system with its patchwork of welfare schemes and state control.

This process of collaboration has been aided by the formation of the TUC, which has thrown up a range of formidable statesmen – George Woodcock, Vic Feather, Len Murray – to whom governments have turned for advice and for assistance in managing economic forces. The task of government has been traditionally easier when Labour has been in office, for one major way in which trade unions developed new shoots was in the growth of the Labour Party in the early years of the twentieth century, a party which depended on trade union funds and trade union support, as of course it still does. When that party moved from group pressure for specific reforms, such as the Trades Disputes Act, to the party of government, it inherited problems which were directly to affect trade unions. If the government was a party sprung from trade unions, how far could a working class organised economically challenge the working class organised politically? How far could trade unions justify the calling of strikes which might affect the standing of the government as well as the future of the economy?

The size, wealth and power of the modern trade union in a society like Britain which so precariously depends on the sale of its manufactured goods to ensure its survival have thrown up difficult questions about its role in the modern state. Some countries have solved the problem by setting up a rigid pattern of state control, as in Nazi Germany or Francoist Spain; others by allowing free trade unions within a network of stringent laws restricting the right to strike and providing a series of alternative procedures, as in contemporary Sweden or in Britain under the Conservative Industrial Relations Bill of 1972. Nineteenth-century Britain was aware of the danger and dealt with it by severe laws against combination at the beginning of the century and a slow development of conciliation machinery towards the end. In the years between trade union and employer faced each other within industry, and victory often depended more on the state of the trade or the price of the product than on the genuine needs of both sides or, equally pertinently, the overall needs of society. The dramatic intervention of Gladstone in the mining dispute of 1893 exemplifies the acceptance of responsibility by government for disasters which could affect the whole of society.

Trade unions were often seen in another guise by employers: as a means by which the rightful prerogatives of management were being undermined by men in the industry's employ. In terms of trade union history, industry was in a similar position to the seventeenth-century constitutional history phase and threw up its village Hampdens as well as its Charles Is. How could the concept of a common interest be realised in such an industry as, say, coalmining, where coal owners moved in comfort with the highest in the land while workers grovelled underground and were drowned, gassed, broken and destroyed in the search of a living? Or in early textile mills with machinery which could maim and scalp, revolving unguarded in their midst, where the working day was so long that the human spirit could hardly survive. Strikes under these conditions could almost be seen as a way of striking an attitude, defying authority in the interests of human dignity.

Trade unions grew up to offer protection to working men when the traditional means of protection had grown weak and new institutions were needed if working men were to find ways of maintaining their interests in a rapidly changing society. In the past, the state had partly protected these interests in the Statute of Artificers (1563) [doc. 1] which had given JPs the power to fix wages, taking into account both the general state of the trade and the needs of the employee. Since the 1660s state paternalism had been increasingly undermined although on the very eve of the statute's repeal clothworkers were petitioning the House of Commons to exercise the protection that Statute promised [doc. 2]. In the changed economic climate Parliament was reluctant to use such power and by 1814 the Statute itself was repealed.

Since 1660 the role of the central government had been changing and Parliament was no longer taking a positive and interventionist interest in the economy. Gradually it had come to be accepted that human beings benefited the whole of society if left to their own economic devices. Regulation by state, by guild, by monopoly, by organisation would hamper the free exercise of the capacity for creating wealth which was the mark of contemporary man. Adam Smith's *Wealth of Nations* eloquently made the plea for the end of all state regulation: Jeremy Bentham's analysis of society as best constructed on a model in which human being sought their own form of happiness provided a philosophic justification for the new society.

The change in the theory of the state was accompanied by the very rapid expansion of the English economy. In the last part of the eighteenth century, England made rapid strides in trade and in industry, and particularly in cotton textiles; the factory, an aggregate of workers, began to appear as the normal production unit in cotton. The small-scale production unit based on master and apprentices and journeymen began to give way to another and larger unit. There might still be a family basis in that the owner would still be involved in production but the size of the unit would make it impossible any longer to maintain the fiction that the interests of the worker coincided with those of the owners.

With the state no longer concerned to maintain wages – in 1795 Parliament rejected Whitbread's minimum wage Bill – but merely to provide the framework of public order within which industry, commerce and Englishmen could thrive and prosper, working men began to combine to find ways of fixing their own wages within the new and industrialising society. A union of men to protect and advance their own interests came into existence in many industries; within capitalist society the interests of workmen came to be seen as independent of their employer. The state offered no protection, of working conditions, working hours or rates of pay, for any security against illness, unemployment or death. Trade unions developed to meet these basic needs. The trade society in the past was often a Friendly Society and early trade unions in the industrial age often combined the functions of an insurance scheme and an organisation to improve the lot of members.

The trade union grew up as a means of selfprotection for individual groups of workers: it did not initially conceive of interests being shared within a larger group, a class, rather than one particular skill or trade. Although the debate on the way in which class consciousness grew still goes on **(97, 109, 115)** it might be argued that not until the formation of the Labour Representation Committee (LRC) in 1900 was the time reached when the working class adapted the need for common working class action within the political framework of an independent political party. Within capitalist society the trade union was not seen as a means of sharing power with the employer, or reducing his prerogatives of ownership: its scope was traditionally more limited, perhaps humbler, to secure a reasonable return for labour for its members. Social and economic power rested with the employer; the law favoured his interest during most of the nineteenth century; Parliament rarely concerned itself with the problems of labour. British trade unionism grew with British industry. During the period covered by this book it represented a persistent attempt to secure within a laissez faire society a fair share of the national income from employers reluctant to yield more than a bare minimum to any working man.

Some craft unions which have survived into the twentieth century date from the end of the eighteenth – the Brushmakers (1778) or the London Bookinders (1784) – but there were many trade societies which were much more shortlived. They were born, died or disappeared or were transformed into wider bodies. Typically the craft society would be locally based, often with headquarters at the local pub and fundamentally concerned with friendly society benefits. The craftsman with his slightly better education, his steady employment, his higher wage, would be able to give continuity to his local society. Such continuing societies were found within the printing industry where trade union organisation, based on the chapel, was well advanced by the end of the seventeenth century, with a system of 'solaces' or fines for members who infringed trade union rules. A.E. Musson in his study of the history of a printing union (22) suggests that the printers' 'strong propensity for drink' may well have been 'a most important factor' in the founding of early printing trade unions. This inclination made the choice of a public house a natural step as a meeting place for the printing friendly societies. Printers very early developed the practice of tramp relief. Printers out of work were provided with a travelling document entitling them to financial assistance from fellow-workers in other towns [doc. 8].

One other continuing concern for craft societies was the problem of apprentices taken into the trade. The societies were anxious both to control the number of entrants so that the craft would not be swamped and to ensure that new members would serve the right apprenticeship. From individual centres a craft trade society would spread outward through a district and the practice grew of making agreements, especially wage agreements, which would hold true for the whole district, so that craftsmen would know – as masters also would know – the district rate for the job. This had advantages to employers as well for it implied a guarantee that labour costs would be the same for their competitors as for themselves: there could be no undercutting by cheap labour. Craftsmen had loyalties to their fellow craftsmen, not to their class, and wage rates for workmen not protected by a craft union might be depressingly low, with the distinction between the self-protecting and self-perpetuating 'aristocracy of labour' and the rest of the workforce, clear in terms of standard of living and indeed even in class terms. Non-society men inhabited a different world, belonged to a different subculture.

After 1850 craft unions developed rapidly and many took on that new solidity reflected in the strength of the ASE, the 'New Model' and well-established trade unions were found throughout engineering, iron and steel, building and printing. District societies gave way to national unions, with paid secretaries and a democratic machinery of government in which the Central Executive took over the prerogative of deciding on strike action. Agreements, however, were normally still by district rather than national.

With industrialisation, one other form of union developed which it is possible to see as unions of the semiskilled, the operative unions. Typically they were district unions. They appeared in textiles, where the work skill involved in machine industry merited higher pay and status, and in mining, an industry with many differing and relatively complex operations, and where at the pit face skill, strength and courage all called for additional rewards. In cotton, operative unions drew from sections of the industry rather than from individual mills. In mining, where pits varied in yields and in difficulties of working, a network of local unions grew up, some of which like the Northumberland and Durham Miners' Union remaining intractably local for decades. Local operative unions evolved different wage and work agreements and late nineteenth century union officials were to find difficult the problems of uniting the interests of such widely diverse groups.

With the growth of the TUC after 1868 the craft unions and the operative unions were to dominate the politics of unionism long after the rise of general and industrial unionism. With the formation of the LRC in 1900, the engineers, the textile workers and the miners were still the largest unions and two of these were initially to withhold their support from the new attempt to send labour politicians to Parliament. The tradition of sturdy independence was too strongly held: if MPs were to be sent (and there was by then general agreement on this) it was better that they should represent the interests of individual unions.

As late as the 1880s it was the rare worker whose interests were protected by a trade union. The casual worker on the docks, the unskilled worker, women workers, the shop assistant had no union to bargain for their interests. It might be argued that as long as their labour could readily be replaced a union traditionally concerned with selling skills could not easily grow. But from the 1880s general unions, symbolically, if not actually, beginning with the Dockers and the Gasworkers in 1889, began to develop rapidly, concerned to take in all those workers for whom no unions existed and to secure for them better conditions and better wages. The industrial union, such as the National Union of Railwaymen, was a further development in which an attempt was made to end separate bargaining by different grades and different skills and to set up a union to represent all workers in negotiations with the management.

The final expansion began after 1900. In 1893 there were 1,559,000 trade unionists in 1,279 trade unions: in 1900 there were 2,022,000 in 1,323. There was a slight decline in the early years of the century but by 190 membership had recovered to 2,210,000, reaching 2,565,000 in 1910. From that point membership rapidly increased and by 1914 there were 4,145,000 members. By this time, too, trade unionists had their own central organisation, their own political party, and were immune from action in the courts for losses produced by their members. Again, whereas in some countries such as New Zealand the right to strike had been banned by law, in Britain trade unionists still had a weapon which in certain industries such as mining or transport could put at risk the wellbeing and economy of the country as a whole.

This growth in numbers and the new power which trade unionists could wield led employers to form their own protective associations and to look for alternative sources of labour in a strike, and induced the state to consider ways in which the danger of strikes could be averted by the development of conciliation machinery.

2 Trade Unions and the Combination Laws

The French Revolution reached out to affect the lives of many who lived far beyond the frontiers of France and well outside the reach of the yeast of its political ideas. In England Burke trumpeted against its implicit rationalism and property owners became convinced that the very basis of English society was under threat. With that English gift for misunderstanding the nature of continental movements, the English government and the landowning class saw in the Revolution a major spur to the formation of combinations of workmen whose wage claims had clear political overtones. Yet the French Revolution offered no immediate model for trade union organisation — its initial goals were purely political and social. Indeed the Assembly in *le loi Chapelier (1791)* had specifically prohibited industrial combinations. In the political theory of the bourgeois revolutionaries, combination inhibited freedom and to revolutionary thought freedom was fundamental, the freedom preached by Adam Smith and the whole school of British liberals whose attitude to combination was similar to the founding fathers of the Revolution.

Political combinations there certainly were: groups such as the Corresponding Societies seeking to come to intellectual terms with the Revolution and Tom Paine, but such groups were far removed from the trade societies, artisans bargaining for wage increases against a background of steeply rising prices. In the critical period, 1791–94, letters piled on to the desk of the Home Secretary, Henry Dundas, evidencing the alarm felt by the rural magistracy [doc. 3] that the agitations and combinations in the provinces were the preliminary rumblings of a provincial revolution similar to that which France had undergone, and that the raw material was there from which a revolutionary situation might develop. What might in less troubled times have been considered grossly inflated wage demands came rapidly to be dubbed Jacobinical, carrying a grave threat to the social order. When war against revolutionary France began in 1793, the wage claims of the trade societies were seen for what they were: clear evidence of disaffection. To workmen caught in the grip of inflation, worsened by a war economy based on loans, this bargaining was no more than a means of keeping afloat in a rapidly changing situation.

The common law of England already had sufficient legal weapons to deal with any subversive claims from workingmen. Combination 'in restraint of trade' was an indictable offence, conspiracy, and punishments could be severe. To strengthen the law, employers in different trades had secured the passing of separate statutes to deal with workmen's combinations. The notorious 1799 Combination Law arose from just such a proposal. The London master millwrights petitioned the Commons to prohibit combinations within their own trade and William Wilberforce eloquently condemned combinations as 'a general disease in our society'. The call was for comprehensive legislation and Pitt introduced a government Bill to prohibit combinations.

No new principle was introduced by the Combination Act. Its declared aim was to prevent 'unlawful combinations of workmen', yet combinations were already unlawful. The application of existing law could be very slow, for due process required the procedures of the Assize courts. What the new Act offered was summary trial before a Justice of the Peace, a relatively speedy means of dealing with recalcitrant workmen. Often the mere threat of legal prosecutions under the Act was sufficient to still a wage demand. The amendment in 1800 allowed appeals to the Court of Quarter Sessions, thereby taking a little of the sting out of the practice of summary jurisdiction. Judged by contemporary standards, penalties were remarkably light: three months imprisonment was the maximum, whereas under existing legislation the maximum was seven years transportation. Two interesting provisions formed part of the Combination Laws – a clause forbidding employers' combinations and a clause providing for arbitration in wage disputes, with a legal obligation binding both parties to the award.

The Webbs (25) saw the Combination Laws as 'a far-reaching change of policy, producing in the first twenty years of the nineteenth century a legal persecution of trade unionists as rebels and unionists'. For the Hammonds (26) the laws were 'the most unqualified surrender of the state to the discretion of a class in the history of England'; Aspinall, despite his general defusing of the acts, concurs with this judgement and dubs them 'an odious piece of class legislation'; Dorothy George (78) shares the opinion of George White, the parliamentary agent who drafted the 1824 repeal, and sees the Laws as 'a very negligible instrument of oppression', a view shared by A.E. Musson (27). E.P. Thompson points to the interesting paradox that 'it was in the very years when the Acts were in force that trade unionism registered great advances' (76).

Although as yet there has been insufficient investigation into the effect of the Combination Laws on different trades and industries, historians are in general agreement that while employers were anxious to have them placed on the statute book, they were not widely used.

Indeed more often the older laws against combinations were invoked, and in some industries employers preferred to turn a blind eye to the existence of combinations. On occasion even magistrates tried to avoid interfering in industrial disputes, as for instance in the protracted Manchester cotton spinners strike in 1818.

The Combination Laws form part of English political history, symbolising the extreme reaction of a conservative government to the anticipated dangers from France, and particularly the potent infection of French political ideas. When, with the defeat of France, that danger disappeared, the Laws came to be regarded as 'almost a dead letter' as the Home Office pointed out in 1818 (72). That interpretation is given support by Cole's essay on the attempts to create a General Union, which saw 1818 as a starting date, and by the widespread strike activity of that year.

After sixteen years, observes Henry Pelling (29) 'combinations were at least as widespread as before and probably more so'. The attitude of magistrates and employers had been only one of several factors which account for this. Trade unions had taken advantage of the improved postal services to keep in touch with other groups in other parts of the country. From Freemasonry they had learnt the techniques of secret societies and from Methodism the model of delegation, representation and federation. From the Hampden Clubs they had adopted their giant waving, carefully woven banners and the value of dramatic, colourful processions with banners held high. Pub landlords providing meeting places, security of funds and beer for the officials.

In textiles in particular there had been rapid unionisation. Before the advent of the factory craft societies had common objectives, prevention of the use of blacklegs in a turn-out, control of apprentices, the closed shop. The new skilled men in the cotton industry, the spinners, quickly adopted the traditional pattern of organisation and a similar band of objectives to the existing trade societies. Such a new but traditional union was the Stockport and Manchester Spinning Society, established in 1792, and similar industrial patterns appeared in the woollen industry. In a fairly static economic society such trade unions were able to defend their members' interests reasonably well, indeed the Lancashire spinners' societies tried not only to enforce apprenticeship but also to limit it to the children of members or the children of friends. The rapidly changing industrial society of early nineteenth-century England with its spate of new and small companies made these trade unions more precarious and produced a change in objectives. In the major strike of spinners in 1810 the demand was for 'equalisation of wages' to bring all wages in the Lancashire area from Stockport to Preston, Oldham and Bolton up to the level paid by the best firms. The strike lasted four months before it was finally defeated.

The 1810 strike had been costly, nearly £1,500 was paid out in strike benefits at the rate of 12 shillings a week to strikers and the loss of funds made strike action unlikely for many years to come, for the current level of wages did not make it easy to accumulate sufficient capital to support a further strike.

In 1818 another major strike took place in the cotton industry, which involved weavers as well as spinners. Beginning in Stockport with the spinners the strike quickly spread to the powerloom weavers and the local magistrates arrested the leaders. From this initial strike developed an attempt, the first, to set up a General Union of Trades. (30) The Lancashire men made contact with the London shipwrights and the Spitalfields silk weavers and subsequently a range of skilled workers such as colliers, hatters, bricklayers, shoemakers, machine makers. An organisation was to be established with a monthly delegate meeting charged with the responsibility of considering all wage demands. This was the body known as the 'Philanthropic Society' and in London a similar broad-based society appeared, the 'Philanthropic Hercules'. This early attempt to forge working-class unity across a range of trades was destroyed by the arrest of five members of the Spinners' Committee. Despite its brief life, this attempt at a general union is of interest as the first attempt to co-ordinate working-class policies in the face of the often hostile and repressive conditions of early industrial England.

By the early 1820s most of the techniques of repression had been dismantled and the Combination Laws were archaic in a society where government was reforming penal law and trying to lift some restrictions on trade. The Repeal of the Combination Laws reflects the new ideas of the new men, particularly Robert Peel, who commented: 'Men who have no property except their manual skill and strength, ought to be allowed to confer together, if they think fit, for the purpose of determining at what rate they will sell their property.' The new liberal ideas flowing from the work of Adam Smith and Jeremy Bentham affected the common attitude to the Laws. Francis Place, a man of sound Benthamite economic views, worked hard for repeal on the mistaken assumption that repeal would reduce the need for combinations and it was he who persuaded Joseph Hume, a fellow Radical and Member of Parliament, to have a Select Committee of Inquiry set up. The Select Committee found that the Combination Laws served 'to produce mutual irritation and distrust' and 'to give a violent character to the Combinations'. They recommended, together with repeal of all statutes against peaceful combinations, a change in the common law relating to combinations.

V.L. Allen (72) is critical of the emphasis usually placed on the activities of Francis Place. What is significant, he argues, is not the work of individuals but 'the conditions which led to such a repeal'. In his view also 'their removal from the Statute Book in 1824 like the removal of so much legislation, came long after they had lost their utility'.

Place's confident predictions of declining interest in combinations was confounded by the events of 1824 (2). Instead of trade unions virtually disappearing in the new liberal era, there was, against a background of a rapid upturn in trade, an immediate expansion of trade unionism, coupled with strikes, with demands for closed shops, and occasionally with violence. An alarmed Parliament hurriedly passed an Amending Act (1825) restricting the purpose of combinations.

Overall the statutory changes of 1824-25 had made fundamental gains for trade unions. They were now legal and they were free to carry on essential trade union activities – they could collect union dues, engage in collective bargaining, and, if necessary, go on strike. However, trade union funds were still unprotected by law and trade unionsts could still be sued for breach of contract or for action in restraint of trade. Workmen were not allowed to picket, 'molest' or 'obstruct' in pursuit of trade union objectives, and these offences carried sentences of up to three months in prison. Again, although collective bargaining was now legal, employers continued to resist this means of reaching agreement with their workers. The technique they used was 'The document' [doc. 6], a declaration forced on the worker, agreeing not to join a trade union. Despite their still equivocal position and the hostility of many employers, trade unions in the late 1820s developed ambitiously, not only with the unionisation of particular trades, but also with attempts at general unions of all the trades.

The Rise of the Unions

PART TWO

The Rise of the Unions

3 The Struggle for Recognition

LOCAL AND GENERAL UNIONISM

In the early nineteenth century working-class movements took many forms, of which the trade union, a combination of workers to negotiate, to strike and to protect, was only one. Luddism and its later variants, what E.J. Hobsbawm calls 'collective bargaining by riot' **(107)** was another, organisations of workers to protect living standards threatened by catastrophic decline by the introduction of new machinery in labour intensive industries. (The plight of the weavers, a class without any means of protection, has been charted movingly by E.P. Thompson **(76)**). Friendly societies providing insurance against sickness and death were other institutions which the English working class developed, often combining these functions with established trade unions. In the two decades after 1830, workers' concern for the position of their class in English society, denied political rights, was also expressed in political societies such as the National Union of the Working Classes, or the most highly organised of all, the Chartist Movement, which dominated the politics of the late 1830s and the 1840s. Such a brief survey does not cover the many other movements and institutions which sprang up, Short-Time Committees, Anti-Poor Law Committees or Land Schemes. In the changing industrial landscape of the period there was room for many diverse organisations, without there necessarily being strong links between them.

In the Webbs' account of the 1830s and 1850s, the contrast is strongly drawn between the generous and impracticable universalism of the Owenite and Chartist organisations and the principle of protection of the vested interests of the craftsman in his occupation. In the 1830s came the false dawn of the Grand National, and then in the 1850s, the solid British worth of the new model, the Amalgamated Society of Engineers.

Such a contrast is more misleading than illuminating. The 1830s had its existing craft societies, the 'honourable' men, the 'society' men, the labour aristocracy working for the agreed wage after the appropriate apprenticeship, whose worklives were markedly different from the 'dishonourables', the 'illegals', workers who where not members of the society. The society men shared the basic trade union

17

concerns which came to typify the new model and they represent the continuing thread in the history of trade unionism. To a very large extent they remained untouched by the Grand National, which mainly gathered its support from those outside the existing trade union structure, moving into virgin fields such as the farm labourers and the less skilled or unskilled members of other trades. Owenism and Chartism did not activate existing trade societies, rather both movements brought in new groups mainly outside the trade societies.

Trade union activity in the 1820s was normally found in trade societies which were small and local, although the loose federation of the printers could be found in several trades such as engineering, where 'tramping' was common [doc. 8]. The need for links and for reciprocal agreements remained strong and became easier to organise with the new postal service and the growing rail network. In engineering, where industrial developments were rapid and men were being sent from town to town to work on assembling new machines or servicing existing plant, unions such as the Journeymen Steam Engine Makers, founded in the 1820s had branches in more than one town. There were also stirrings of unionism among the miners in Cheshire, Staffordshire, Yorkshire and South Wales, and some of the more militant mining unions gave their support to John Doherty's attempt at a general union in 1829.

Movements for a general union as G.D.H. Cole has shown (30) go back to before the Repeal of the Combination Laws, to 1818 and the attempt to create a 'Philanthropic Hercules' in London and the 'Philanthropic Society' in Lancashire, both of which were intended to create a loose federation of industrial workers, and although shortlived, represent a pattern for later attempts, of which the Grand National is the most famous.

Ten years later a fresh impulse for a more general form of union reappeared when in 1829 the able and energetic John Doherty, after founding a Cotton Spinners Union in Manchester, called a conference [doc. 4] (in the Isle of Man) to establish a Grand General Union of the Operative Spinners of Great Britain and Ireland. From this base he extended into the creation of a general union bringing in Staffordshire potters and other local trade clubs into the National Association for the Protection of Labour. The NAPL found support outside Lancashire, in Birmingham, Huddersfield and Newtown, Montgomeryshire. It proved unable effectively to call its members out on strike to oppose a wage reduction imposed by the master spinners in the Ashton-under-Lyne district and its strength declined until its virtual disappearance in 1832.

An earlier attempt at a general union was made in the building industry when in 1827 a General Union of Bricklayers and Carpenters was set up, to be transformed into the Operative Builders Union in 1832. This body ran the affairs of its members in a Builders' Parliament which met twice yearly to work out policy for all the building operatives.

One major difference between the spinners and builders lay in the aims of the union. Doherty had set himself in the NAPL the limited aim of collecting dues from members to finance a strike whenever employers forced wage reductions (a limited aim which in the event proved difficult to achieve). The Operative Builders' Union was deeply affected by Owenism. Raymond Postage quotes (18) their objective as concerned 'to organise the great working mass of Builders in the Kingdom as to place them in a permanent position of comfort and happiness – and to destroy that ruinous system of competition . . . which has reduced them to misery'.

From this splendid vision grew the Builders' Union, based on Manchester, Birmingham and London, all three major centres of building trades unionism. Its General Council, the Builders' Parliament, met in September 1833 and called for the creation of a Grand National Guild of Builders with a proposed membership of around 60,000. The new union would provide all the traditional friendly society benefits offered by the trade societies and extend into education and medicine and also offer immediate competition to the master builders by entering into direct building contracts. The intended membership would be comprehensive, running from architects through bricklayers and all other skilled members of the trade. A hope was expressed that the lower end of the trade, 'quarriers, brickmakers and labourers', would be granted membership just as soon as 'they can be prepared with better habits and more knowledge to enable them to act for themselves, assisted by other branches who will have an overwhelming interest to improve the mind, morals and general condition of their families in the shortest time'.

The scroll placed under the foundations of the Union Institute in Brimingham struck an optimistic note. 'In a confident hope', it proudly read, 'of success, this work is commenced, being, as it is believed, the beginning of a new era in the condition of the whole of the working classes of the world.'

Despite this apocalyptic tone, the builders did not join the Grand National Consolidated Trades Union. Nor did they outlive their larger and more comprehensive competitor, for they were brought down by the famous 'beer dispute'. Their original quarrel was with the London brewers, Combe, Delafield, who refused to employ trade unionists and the builders employed by Cubitts, the London building firm, who boy-cotted Combe Delafield's non-union beer. Cubitts moved into this dispute by providing only this brewer's beer in the building yards under their control, thus at one stroke requiring builders to drink Combe's or none at all. The matter took a serious turn when the dispute broadened into a lockout, with many of the London builders involved. The confrontation now involved The Document [doc. 6] on the employers' side, and on the union's side a demand for uniformity of wage rates and the dismissal of all non-unionists. The protracted struggle brought about the dissolution of the Builders' Union. Individual unions, such as stone-masons, plumbers, carpenters, went on in their own way, although some unions, such as the plasterers and the slaters, were extinguished entirely (18).

The culmination of movements for a general union was clearly the Grand National [doc, 5], which should be seen, not only as within the sequence which began in 1818 but within the context of the 1830s, as forming one aspect of that wide working-class movement, reflected in a whole range of different activities from political reform groups like the National Union of the Working Class to short-time committees and committees set up to oppose the hated Poor Law. New industries, new towns, new forms of action, new hopes, helped to produce the Grand National. The response of government, too, has to be seen against the background of agricultural distress and the Captain Swing riots, apprehension about the taking of secret oaths, the apparent danger that the rural population would be politicised by urban militants, and the renewed fear that the very framework of society was once more in danger.

The Grand National had its origins in the attempt by Derby employers to destroy combinations in the local trades. The Derby workers appealed to London for help, a call which brought into existence the conference from which the Grand National sprang. How far was this general union a reflection of the ideas of Robert Owen, prophet and critic of the new social order he saw emerging in the nineteenth century? By any standards Robert Own was a remarkable man. Born in 1771 at Newtown, Montgomeryshire, the son of a postmaster, he rose by his native energy and a judicious marriage to be the owner of the textile mills at New Lanark, south of Glasgow, which he bought from his father-in-law, David Dale.

Owen's fundamental criticism of the new society which emerging industrialisation was creating was contained in the series of essays published in 1817, *A New View of Society*, which bitterly attacked the impact of industrialisation upon certain vulnerable groups such as children and also offered the prospect of an alternative form of social and industrial organisation. In Owen's new society competition was to give way to cooperation, the total environment was to be changed so that man would shed his competitive characteristics and become the new man concerned to work in harmony for improvement. At his factory in New Lanark Owen experimented with a new industrial and social environment, with welfare and educational schemes which made his factory a meeting place for European reformers. The principle of cooperation applied to working men would within capitalist society imply complete unionisation, which would in turn offer alternative means by which industry could be organised. That the Grand National can be seen as a nationwide attempt to carry Owen's ideas into practice is very doubtful: it was an attempt to set up a union broadly representing the interests of all the trade societies it comprised. The member unions were still primarily concerned with problems of wages in their own industries.

A.E. Musson (71) argues 'that Owen's utopian, pacifist ideas, were unacceptable to most trade unionists, who were more interested in a general union for supporting strikes', a concern which would put the GNCTU [doc. 5] well within the tradition of Doherty's National Association. However Musson also points out that 'the extreme militant plan for a "grand national holiday", or general strike, also failed to win any widespread support'.

The Webbs have told us that 'within a few weeks the Union appears to have been joined by at least half a million members, including tens of thousands of farm labourers and women'. This estimate has been rejected by W.H. Oliver (79) who gives the figure of 16,000 as the total paid up membership, but the distinction may lie in those who joined and those who were sympathisers and the GNCTU might in this sense be seen as a 'movement' rather than a formal trade union organisation.

Robert Owen was not a member of the conference which set up in the GNCTU although after the Dorchester trial he became President. Owenite influence could be seen in schemes for settling workmen on the land, or in the proposal to set up cooperative production units manned by men on strike (30, 51). Local branches, however informal, were set up of cordwainers, sawyers, stove makers, gas stokers and others, and the formation of a branch was often followed by strike action to improve wages and conditions. The invasion of the countryside by the GNCTU was too direct threat in troubled conditions of rural England. *The Times* called for action and Melbourne, as Home Secretary, invoked the 1797 Act against unlawful oaths; and the luckless six labourers of Tolpuddle in Dorset were sentenced to seven years transportation. The country rang with trade union protest and London saw the first massive trade union procession, carrying on this occasion a petition to the Prime Minister, Lord Melbourne. The Six Men of Dorset, the Tolpuddle Martyrs, gave to trade union history clear evidence of the repressive means that state power could employ against organisations of working men.

The GNCTU found its main support among the London tailors and shoemakers. It failed to bring in the well-established trade societies such as the printers or engineers who continued to make unspectacular progress of the town-by-town and craft-by-craft type both during and after the events of 1834. The Grand National did not bring in the northern unions such as the cotton spinners. It suffered from inadequate finance; it was aiming to unionise those outside the traditional societies. It may readily be seen as something too ambitious, yet what is also true is that it set itself the traditional trade union objective of protecting its members against deterioration of wages and conditions, and, as the Webbs point out, 'it found itself incessantly involved in sectional disputes for small advances of wages and reductions of hours'. For joining the union workers were sacked or locked out. Their desperation may perhaps be glimpsed in the Derby lockout, which ran for four months before the defeated workers abandoned their union and returned to work.

Everywhere the employer, faced with union membership, presented The Document [doc. 6], and their superior economic power defeated the GNCTU. Employers and government combined to oppose the union and after 1834 large-scale defensive combinations were no longer possible. The immediate future lay with the well-established trade societies, the 'Old Model'. How far did these trade societies support political action such as the Chartist movement of the late 30s and the 40s? The precise relationship between Chartism and trade unionism has produced a major debate between historians. The basic question turns on the existence of 'that pendulum swing between economic action through trade unions and political action' postulated by Asa Briggs (44), a view summarised by J.F.C. Harrison in this way (73): 'For the time being [in the 1840s] Chartism seemed to offer better hope of advancement than trade unionism, and the new cause with the more urgent dynamic absorbed the energies of its predecessor.' But which trade unions, and which trade unionists?

The Webbs held that 'there is no reason to believe that Trade Unions at any time became part and parcel of the Movement ... though some of their members furnished the most ardent supporters of the

Charter'. O'Connor in the *Northern Star* in 1846, in criticising the 'criminal apathy' of the trade societies, bears out the Webbs' view. I. Prothero **(98, 99)** tell us in his article on London Chartism that there was a great overlapping of personnel, although he qualifies this in a later article by concluding that 'weaker unions were in general more likely to be interested in political activity'. D.J. Rowe **(100)** identifies in London such groups as shoemakers and stonemasons as strong Chartist supporters and he says of the Chartist trade societies which were set up that they were 'very peaceful organisations . . . having little or no effect on the general working populace of London', and 'insufficiently powerful to create a thriving metropolitan Chartism'.

During this early period the growth of trade unions must be considered as part of the general development of the working-class movements of the time, as one of the many means by which working-class men tried to advance their interests within the new society. Effective unions were extremely difficult to organise and to maintain. Many jobs, particularly on the land or in domestic industry, called for only minimal skills and entry was therefore easy and discontented workers could readily be replaced. Neither here nor even in the industries based on traditional skills was continuous trade unionism easy, for in industries such as engineering new technology was bringing in rapid changes and endangering the very skills which the unions had been established to protect. Again, the rapid expansion of population, augmented by the flow of Irish immigrants, had created a mobility of labour of great utility in strike-breaking. Furthermore the general fluctuations of industry, with its periodic troughs of depression, had impeded the natural growth of trade unionism and made the task of maintaining the standard of living even more difficult for members of the established societies. The hostility of the law could still be invoked, dramatically as in 1834, with exile as the punishment, and in the continual harassment implicit in the employers' privileged position in the contractual relations between man and master where a breach of contract by the worker could still lead to prison. That trade societies did survive is evidence both of industrial courage and of industrial need.

THE 'NEW MODEL'
The rapid growth in engineering and the changes in the structure of the industry provided the backcloth against which the 'new model' appeared. At the beginning of the nineteenth century, engineering consisted mainly of making steam engines for the textile industry and bridge building, both of which depended on skilled, basically itinerant,

craftsmen, formed into local trade societies. The 'making of machines by machines' (20) was to site engineering in a factory, throw up new skills and new societies. The development of the machine tool industry in the first part of the nineteenth century, the invention by Henry Maudslay of the new lathe, the development of screw-cutting by machine, produced a proliferation of skills: pattern makers, iron and brass founders, turners, planers and smiths.

At first employers thought that the new machines would only require machine-minders and that they would be able to reduce the wage costs which the old well-paid millwrights had established. This proved to be an unfounded hope and the new factories with their concentration of skilled men became the forcing ground of new trade societies — new compared with the old millwrights, the traditional engineering craftsman, but with industrial aims not markedly dissimilar to the older craftsmen and concerned with regulation of overtime, restriction of entry, the serving of apprenticeships and with the equally traditional pattern of mutual assistance.

One such society, was the Friendly Union of Mechanics, founded in 1826 in Manchester, which united with the Yorkshire Mechanics' Friendly Society in 1838 to become the Journeymen Steam Engine and Machine Makers' Friendly Society, a title extended in 1842 to include the Millwrights. This new union (often called 'the Old Mechanics') covered the textile-machinery-makers of the North and was fiercely protective of the status of members against the threat of the 'illegals'. This pattern of accretion or federation may be observed in other skilled worker unions; in printing, a union covering Lancashire and Yorkshire and extending to the Welsh border counties, emerged in 1830: the Northern Typographical Union, from which in 1844 was forged the National Typographical Association.

In two important respects the 'Old Mechanics' broke new ground: first by appointing in 1845 a full-time paid secretary, the able and vigorous Robert Robinson, and secondly in its militant campaign against the technique used by northern employers against trade unions, the 'quittance paper'. The quittance paper was a workman's identity card, a passport to future employment which set out his leaving wage rate, his employer's opinion of him and his reasons for leaving. To defeat this practice, the 'Old Mechanics' in 1844 set up the Mechanics' Protective Society of Great Britain and Ireland, with strong centres in Manchester, Liverpool, Bury and Bolton, and mounted defensive strikes against employers using the quittance paper.

Joint action against employers proved successful and the practice was stopped. Such a precedent seemed useful in the crisis of 1846. A strike which had been called in an engineering firm in Newton-le-Willows, led to the arrest of Henry Selsby, the general secretary and twenty-six other members. Charged with 'unlawfully conspiring' the union appeared to be at great risk, and the danger was confirmed when Selsby and others were found guilty, a judgment which was rescinded on appeal. Some union members wanted to retreat to a passive and local policy but William Newton of London and William Allan of Crewe argued for a further increase in strength (the union now had nearly 7000 members) by amalgamating with other engineers in the industry.

The initiative of Allan and Newton led to the calling of joint conferences to amalgamate existing unions, and in 1851 the Amalgamated Society of Engineers, Machinists, Smiths, Millwrights and Pattern-makers was born [doc. 7]. Its policies differed little from the 'Old Mechanics', except in its insistence on regarding the need for strike pay to be raised by a levy on members rather than by voluntary contributions. Indeed opposition within the Old Mechanics turned to a very great extent on Newton's assumption that there would be further strikes, and if there were they must be won. In most other respects, in its opposition to systematic overtime, on the need to keep apprentices down to a ratio of 1 to 4, the Amalgamated Society of Engineers reflected faithfully the industrial ideals of its predecessor. The new body took over William Allan (who had succeeded Selsby in 1848) as general secretary but made the major departure of centring its headquarters in London.

A.E. Musson has argued that 'what occurred in the fifties and sixties was not the creation of a "New Model" but a strengthening of the old' (71). V.L. Allen sees 'New Model' unionism as a piece of historical fiction (80).

Certainly the ASE looks more like a traditional trade society than a completely new departure. Its novelty, perhaps, lies in its siting in a new and expanding industry where the threat of 'illegals' was greater and where the creation of new techniques continually threw up problems of hierarchy and dilution rather than in the more traditional and less revolutionary industries of mining or building.

The ASE by the 1860s was reluctant to strike, at a time when membership and funds were growing and the standard of living was rising. Strikes had to be approved by the Executive Council, which was slow to give its approval. But this apparent lack of militancy reflected more the state of trade in the 1860s and the craft engineer's satisfaction with his lot rather than any inbuilt opposition to strikes in themselves as the evidence of the 1852 strike demonstrates. The ASE's challenge to the employers turned on their opposition to piecework and to overtime.

On 1 January 1852 the union called for a ban on both these practices. As Keith Burgess (82) has shown it was the large firms (employing more than fifty) in both Lancashire and London who responded by ordering a lockout of their workforce. On the other hand, the labour-intensive small firm usually accepted the ASE's demands. The struggle with the large firms ended with defeat for the union, despite the £12,000 collected from members not affected by the strike and lockout. The defeat ended with ASE members in large firms forced to accept the document. In this collision the ASE was fighting for traditional objectives within the new industrial context of a capital intensive industry. For owners whose capital had been sunk in the new screwmaking machines it was essential to keep the machines working.

The defeat of the ASE by the employers lost the new amalgamated society some of its members. Within the union William Newton argued persuasively for cooperative workshops as the logical next step, a policy which the general secretary considered marginal. In his view the ASE must make up lost ground, build up its membership, and create a strong union with a consequent growth in bargaining power. And when Parliament in the late 1860s began to survey British trade union organisation, Allan's policy made the ASE the premier union, powerful, respectable and considered by its Liberal friends as evidence of working-class capacity for adaptability to advancing Victorian capitalism – in every sense a new model, trade unionism without conflict or confrontation.

Engineering and building might be seen to typify the great expansionist industries of mid-Victorian England, and in building, as in engineering, a new union structure developed after a major confrontation – the nine-hour-day movement in 1859 – and the new unions adopted 'new model' policies. The campaign for a nine-hour day began as early as 1853 and was sharpened by the building recession of 1858-59. There had been no similar growth in the size of the enterprise: building remained the province of the small firm, with techniques not markedly mechanised. A reduction in working hours seemed to offer to building workers both a means of safeguarding living standards and dealing with unemployment in the industry. George Howell, a building trade union organiser, observed 'The Nine Hours Movement was the starting point for other movements, some of which have left their mark on the political as well as the industrial history of the country.' Certainly from this struggle emerged a more politically conscious leadership amongst the artisans, such as builders and carpenters, who were most immediately affected (18).

The nine-hour day became the key issue in the famous stoppage in the London building trades in 1859. The struggle began at the South London building firm of Trollope's in Pimlico when a trade unionist was dismissed after presenting a petition for a reduction of an hour a day. The dismissed man had been one of a delegation of building workers and the delegation had been one of four who had simultaneously presented petitions to four different London firms.

All the Trollope workmen came out on strike. The building trade employers met this collective action by locking out all building workers throughout London. The two sides settled down to the prospect of a long-drawn-out battle. The union side had a phalanx of masons and bricklayers, all of whom, backed up by a new union, the Builders' Labourers' Union and buttressed by other trade societies from outside the dispute, including the ASE, who gave £3,000 to the strike fund. The trade societies asked for reinstatement and the nine-hour day. On their side the employers revived The Document [doc. 6] in an attempt to destroy all trade union organisation within the building industry in London.

From November 1859 until February 1860 this struggle went on before finally a compromise was agreed; the employers withdrew The Document and the men abandoned the nine-hour day. On the workers' side the struggle brought out the need for a permanent collective organisation of the London building industry. The Builders' Strike Committee was directly responsible for the special trade society conference setting up the London Trades Council, a move towards the coordination of trade union interests and towards providing a forum for discussion of matters of common interest. There was one other important result: the adaptation by the carpenters of the model offered by the ASE in the Amalgamated Society of Carpenters in 1860, a union which under the careful guidance of Robert Applegarth, its general secretary from 1862, was to rival the ASE in power and influence.

During the struggle George Potter emerged as spokesman and organiser; he was secretary of the Joint Committee. He was to use his experience on a larger stage with the founding in 1861 of the *Beehive*, one of the most influential of all radical newspapers (**89**). He was to continue the struggle for a nine-hour day by calling a conference in Derby from which sprang the United Kingdom Association for Shortening the Hours of Labour in the Building Trades. Potter was secretary and again the struggle centred on London. One member of the strike committee who later became famous was George Howell, who had during the previous strike become a member of the bricklayers' union. The strike ran altogether for several months and Howell became a prominent militant, negotiating, writing articles, visiting pickets. The financial strength of the union was impressive. They spent in all £1,850 during the strike, and Howell and fellow members of the strike committee were paid around 35 shillings a week. The strikers were once more defeated and they returned to work on the employers' terms of an hourly not a daily rate. Again from this struggle emerged a new London based trade union, the Bricklayers, with a constitution, a full-time secretary annually elected, and a policy directly concerned with friendly society benefits and travelling relief.

In these three unions – the Amalgamated Society of Engineers, the Amalgamated Carpenters and the Operative Bricklayers Society – lay the strength of what came to be identified as 'New Model Unionism', but in a famous article (81) G.D.H. Cole has shown how little influence the London-based New Model actually had on trade union development in the Midlands and North. Localism remained the rule through a whole range of crafts: coachbuilding, boot and shoe manufacture, glass and glass bottle making, with some trades such as pottery organised as 'a local centralised society in the Staffordshire area'.

Trade union membership was still only the prerogative of the minority of workers. In most trades membership was the exception not the rule. Mayhew's 10 per cent of the London craft workers is a well-known estimate from a particularly shrewd and knowledgeable observer. In evidence before the 1867 Commission of Inquiry, Alfred Mault, secretary to a Midlands builders' association, gave roughly similar figures: 10 per cent of carpenters, 19 per cent of bricklayers and rather less than 10 per cent of plumbers. But in the twenty years after 1850 most unions grew steadily in membership. Two examples may suffice: the Operative Stonemasons had 4,671 members in 1850 and by 1876 had more than 16,000 members; the ASE had risen from 12,000 to nearly 45,000 in 1880.

In size the ASE was a giant. Judged by the standards of the Victorian success ethic, the ASE was a very trim and well managed ship. The friendly society benefits (with which Applegarth made such play before the Commission) were generous and comprehensive, covering unemployment, sickness, pension and death benefits. Its only rival in insurance cover was the far smaller ASCJ, modelled on the ASE in every respect. Other societies differed widely from each other in the benefits they offered, but in general, sickness benefit was rare. As W.H. Fraser (37) comments; 'In 1880 the majority of unions still lacked a significant benefit side.'

THE LABOUR ARISTOCRACY

The Webbs refer to 'an aristocracy of skilled workmen' and comment on 'the spirit of exclusiveness' which they suggest has had 'an equivocal effect' on the history of the trade union movement. This 'aristocracy', centred on the craft societies such as the ASE, has been seen as class traitors, putting their own interests before those of the class they belonged to, as workers taking on middle-class attitudes and objectives, and as men who sacrificed working-class interests to the narrower group to which they belonged. Fundamentally the labour aristocracy is identified as emerging in the more settled age of advancing Victorian capitalism, in the second half of the nineteenth century.

In his discussion of the labour aristocracy, Hobsbawm **(109)** finds that membership depends on six different characteristics, of which the most important is 'the level and regularity of a worker's earnings' and another is that he 'should be treated with some respect and dignity by employers and to have some freedom of choice in his job'. In his view it 'is doubtful whether we can speak of a labour aristocracy' in the period up to the 1840s; yet the class he describes seems to have much in common with the artisans of the first part of the nineteenth century, indeed of the last part of the eighteenth century also, of whom E.P. Thompson observes that 'the artisans aspired to an "independence", nurturing a dream of becoming a small master' **(76)**.

Mayhew's mid-century survey of the London working classes does much to support the view that profound differences in status, wages and objectives existed amongst the subcultures making up Victorian working-class life. He divided the London population into four classes: those who will work, those who cannot work, those who will not work and those who need not work. The typical trade society was made up from a small section in the first category. Mayhew suggests that only one in ten in any trade are members of a trade society (although Musson working on the same evidence suggests that one in five or one in six would be more accurate **(22)**. These are the true members of the labour aristocracy, earning perhaps twice as much as fellow-workers in the same industry. The bulk of these relative aristocrats came from the old established industries and were compositors, jewellers, watchmakers, ironmoulders, carpenters, shipwrights and others. Early industrialisation had created new groups like the cotton spinner, and later the train driver.

The division between society member and others in the same trade was profound: in earnings, conditions, security of employment, in union membership. It ran right across the grain of their lives, the pubs they went to and their social ambitions, which often resembled those of the lower middle class, concerned with savings, ownership of property and a settled existence. Outside this class, were most of the working classes, the non-society men, the workers who did not belong to a settled trade, such as the navvies building the railway lines and the mass of female workers. In the countryside agricultural workers lived and worked in depressing and humiliating conditions, and groups like the dockers and the sailors and many others depended on the arbitrary benevolence of employers. Mayhew (73) pinpoints the difference in these terms:

The transition from the artisan to the labourer is curious in many respects. In passing from the skilled operative of the west-end to the unskilled workman of the eastern quarter of London, the moral and intellectual change is so great, that it seems as if we were in a new land, and among another race.

The labour aristocracy, then, existed before the 'New Model', indeed the great bulk of trade union activity was found amongst this elite. It would be wrong to attribute to artisan societies any sense of class betrayal, for this would not only be attributing to them a class solidarity which did not exist but also a greater generosity in their loyalties than would be true of other Victorian groups. Carpenters, printers, other skilled men belonged to the skill in which they had been trained; their class loyalties were to that group. They did not spill over into concern for others who had not had the benefit of their special training. In this sense they acted and behaved no differently from, say, barristers, whose concern for their profession would not involved concern for solicitors, who occupied a different social position and had a distinct role. Loyalties were narrow, but no less real for that as the evidence for the widespread practice of tramping shows.

'Socially speaking the best paid stratum of the working class merged with what may be loosely called the "lower middle class"' (Hobsbawm, **109**). Here R. S. Neale's class model for Victorian society (**97**) has implicit relevance because 'the middling class' (lying between two upper and two lower classes on a five-point scale) comprises the petit bourgeois, aspiring professional men and artisans, all of whom Neale sees as a fundamentally non-deferential class. This is to attempt to fit into a sociological model groups who were historically distinct. Artisans were not either lower-middle-class or petit bourgeois; they were working-class. They were not as Neale suggests, concerned with social advancement but with that independence which Thompson stresses in his earlier samples, together with respectability which G. Crossick describes in his survey of the labour aristocracy in Kentish London (Deptford, Greenwich, Woolwich) (115). Richard Hoggart (46) has reminded us of the difference in culture between different streets in a working-class district, the difference between streets with standards and those without. Crossick stressed that the aristocracy were anxious to be seen as 'a respectable body of men' who lived without debts. They differed profoundly from the lower middle classes in three important ways. They were social drinkers. Not only did their trade societies often meet in pubs but so did the friendly societies to which they belonged. Of the eighty-five friendly societies that Crossick examined in Kentish London in 1855-75 all except one met in a public house, a practice frowned on by the lower middle class who were unable to believe that working men, any working man, could control his drinking. Secondly, although independence was the key to their social values, they were not the entirely isolated individuals of the self-help stereotype – they did not reject all help, but help from other classes, which would be charity. Lastly, fundamental to their self-respect was membership of their trade society; even those who became small masters, often retained their membership and therefore their identification with their own class.

The political attitudes of the labour aristocracy can, it is argued (109), be largely understood by their 'shading over' – as a class – into other strata. They tended to be liberal – radical in politics and collaborationist in industrial relations. Trade unions tend to adopt strategies which advance the interests of their members; the 'New Unions' after 1891 developed idiosyncratically, depending on which industry they represented, shaped rather by the situation than any particular doctrine. R.V. Clements in his study of trade union attitudes in the twenty-five years after 1850 (95) quotes from a pamphlet by Thornton Hunt published in 1851 to illustrate what he considers to be 'the constant thread in the nineteenth-century history of the working class'. Thornton Hunt argued for '. . . a fair day's wage for a fair day's work on land, in factory, or shop; the claim to relief from taxation by transferring it from industry to property; and the claim to improvement of the laws regulating labour – the laws of combination, partnership, contracts and the like'. Certainly the ASE and other New Model unions could be seen as following a programme of this kind, through collective bargaining, strikes when needed and a constant recognition that, as Allan put it to the Royal Commission in 1867, 'it is their interest to get the labour at as low a rate as they possibly can, and it is ours to get as high a rate of wages as possible, and you never can reconcile these two things'.

If trade unions were actively collaborating with English capitalism, they did not appear to be when viewed by Charles Dickens or by Samuel Brown, Vice President of Institute of Actuaries who in 1864 saw trade unions as being responsible for 'the interference with the natural adjustment of the rate of wages between masters and workmen' (115). Trade unionists had many lateral links with their own class, through cooperative societies and friendly societies, and the rituals and ceremonies which these societies and their own trade union offered. They worked within the system when that promoted their members' interests as it did clearly in the twenty-odd years after 1850. They became less 'collaborative' after the grim experience of the Great Depression of the 1870s.

What trade societies were offering were dignified lives led at a reasonable level of subsistence: the emphasis on the dignity of membership was to offer a real alternative to the deferential society, and to help to erode, albeit slowly, the social pyramid which made Victorian England so stifling a society for those beneath the higher ranks.

PROVINCIAL UNIONISM

In industrial England's major basic industries, (mining, textiles, iron and steel) conditions differed so much that no common pattern emerged. In mining the localism peculiar to the early stages of English trade unionism was entrenched. Communities were very close and strongly knit and organisation often depended on a single pit. The tendency to create broader organisations, no matter how loosely linked, which acceptance of common problems and common aims forged in many industries, appeared in mining in the form of district unions and occasionally in the setting up of nationwide bodies such as the Miners' Association in 1842. But the conditions in different pits, the nature of the markets in which owners sold their coal, even the form of mining adopted, made localism endemic in mining.

Traditionally, miners were better paid than other workers and lived shorter lives. (In the 1840s they lived ten years less than the national average.) Their problems centred more on conditions, the conditions which killed them off from diseases classified as asthma or consumption, conditions which became the target of the body of mining law which the nineteenth and twentieth centuries have created. Trade societies in mining communities were understandably concerned with providing insurance and friendly society benefits. An early example was the Friendly and Associated Coal Miners within the township of Wakefield, which dates from 1811.

Similar unions existed on some of the other coalfields, but in the smaller pits association was often sporadic and concerned only with immediate problems such as the dilution of the work force by immigrants. One organiser of genius, Tommy Hepburn, built on the base of the Northumberland association of pitmen, first 'Hepburn's Union' in Northumberland, (31) and then a federation of miners in Staffordshire, Yorkshire, Cheshire and Wales. In Northumberland, Hepburn campaigned against the 'Bond', the yearly hiring document, child labour and truck shops, and led a successful strike to reduce the workhours of boys. The employers retaliated by dismissing union labour and hounding Hepburn himself into starvation.

In the 1840s a new wave of militancy swept the pits. Beginning in Wakefield with a call for discussion of matters of general interest, the movement was taken up in the North-East, where in 1843 a meeting of miners' delegates was held in Newcastle-upon-Tyne. From these moves sprang an attempt at a general union of the mining industry, the Miners' Association (83) of Great Britain and Ireland which by 1844 covered 70,000 miners, a third of the nation's miners. Led by Martin Jude, another organiser in the mould of Hepburn, and supported by the great Chartist lawyer W.P. Roberts, a man of passionate eloquence, the Association set itself the long-term objective of improving the standard of living of miners by raising coal prices and restricting output.

On 5 April 1844 the Northumberland and Durham miners withdrew their labour and the owners prepared for a long battle. By the second month of the strike familiar tactics were deployed: blacklegs were imported from Wales and Cornwall and families on strike were evicted to make place for the imported labour. Support for the North-East came from Derbyshire, Nottinghamshire and Yorkshire, and there were strikes of varying length. The strike went on for four bitter months. Strikers' families lived in tents or in improvised huts on the moors, chided by the Marquis of Londonderry, their employer, with what *Punch* called 'epistles of paternal advice' and harassed by his less than paternal attempt to stop food supplies to the strikers by pressure on local shopkeepers. Faced by such provocation the miners remained disciplined and calm until their families reached starvation point and the strike went sour, culminating with attacks on blacklegs and even on their children. Finally the miners' will was broken and they began a slow return to work. In Northumberland one major improvement followed, the abandonment of the Bond, although in the neighbouring Durham coalfields the Bond persisted for another thirty years.

The Miners' Association did not long survive the strike. By 1848 it had disappeared. The Scottish Miners' leader, Alexander Macdonald, speaking in 1873 at the Leeds Miners' Conference, summed up the situation in these words: 'At the close of 1855, it might be said that union . . . had almost died out, the fragments of union got less by degrees and more minute.' To the Webbs this was read as the total extinction of all mining unionism but G.D.H. Cole argues that all Macdonald meant was that 'many lodges ceased to pay dues to any county association, and went their ways as purely independent bodies' (51).

In a comment on Scottish trade unionism S.G. Checkland (40) suggests that this localism was common in Scotland where the national experience ran differently from that in England.

In the revival of unionism from the 1850s Scotland's pattern had been distinctly different from that of England. Instead of strong national unions on the 'New Model' basis, Scotland produced smallish organisations, with a powerful sense of local autonomy, loosely joined together on a federal basis.

It was from this background of localism that Alexander Macdonald, that extraordinary example of Victorian self-help, was to try to create first a Scottish and then nationwide miners' association. After a spell at Glasgow University, where he supported himself by vacation work, he returned to the pits and breathed fresh life into the Scottish Miners' Assocation. From this base, established in 1852, from the platform of the Ashton Miners' Conference, he floated in 1858 the National Miners' Association. A major concern of mining unions was improvement in working conditions by parliamentary intervention, and Macdonald's Association established the pattern for the future in securing the passing of the Coal Mines Regulation Act in 1860, which gave statutory force to the miners' demand for a checkweighman, paid by the miners, to protect the miners from cheating by employers. The checkweighman became the guardian of the men's interests, and inevitably the centre of trade union activity, and because of his position as middleman he guided the union towards moderation and away from militancy.

Macdonald's own concept of mining unions was as moderate pressure groups securing parliamentary backing for gradually improving their conditions and removing their grievances. His influence runs through the 1860 Act to the reform of the Master and Servant Law in 1867 on to the new emerging line of a legally defined eight-hour day. His goal was a national union and he helped to create the National Association of Coal, Limestone and Ironstone Miners' of Great Britain in 1863 (later the National Miners' Union). Its first conference, at Leeds, revealed the continuing strength of regionalism in an industry which structurally encourages strong local loyalties.

Macdonaldism was increasingly opposed by militants, who saw a National Union as a more effective means of dealing with industrial disputes. Cole has pointed out that the irony of this situation (81) is that the principle of centralisation, the 'new model', does not necessarily involve the adoption of moderate policies. Perhaps the explanation for a union's Commitment to a particular line of policy can more readily be found not in the structure of the union but in the nature and state of the industry concerned.

Localism in different degrees persisted on both sides of the textile industry, in weaving and in spinning. Both branches developed trade union organisation, although as their industrial problems were so profoundly distinct, no common organisations covering the industry as a whole ever emerged. In weaving regional associations appeared: a Blackburn-centred federation in 1853 and then a wider grouping, the North-East Lancashire Weavers' Association in 1858. It was almost another thirty years before a county association representing the whole of Lancashire appeared in 1884. Even in the wider associations the principle of localism remained supreme, and only on very rare occasions was there any genuine collective action. Control rested fundamentally with the local society which controlled funds, and therefore policy.

In textile manufacture the spinners could be compared with coalface workers in the pits; in both cases they represented the industry's skilled labour force and the textile spinners organised themselves in a way similar to the butty system in mining. The spinners were fiercely protective of their interests and represented a genuine labour aristocracy. Their overriding concern was to control the size and nature of the workgroup (19), traditionally one spinner to two male assistants, paid by the spinner. One successful struggle carried on by the Spinners' Union had been to prevent the dilution of the trade by female labour. Amalgamations, basically no more than loose federations, were established, but as with the weavers, control of funds, policy and benefits lay with the local society.

In iron and steel one union had had a long history, the Friendly Society of Iron Moulders, changing its name in 1854 to the Friendly Society of Iron Founders. Its general secretary, Daniel Guile, was in office for almost twenty years after 1863, and was a member of the London 'Junta'. The union symbolised the new and moderate, centrally controlled trade union. The expansion of iron and steel helped to create a new society of ironworkers, the Associated Ironworkers in 1863 and from this parent body John Kane's National Amalgamated Association

35

of Ironworkers split off, a union which was to make history of a different kind as a pioneer member of conciliation boards.

4 The Process of Assimilation

TRADES COUNCILS

The growth of vertical organisation in trade unions was paralleled by the emergence of lateral shoots in the new Trades Councils. The New Models, the ASE and the ACSJ helped to found the London Trades Council, and provincial craft unions were foremost in establishing similar bodies in the provinces. Paradoxically from these lateral growths was to appear the new and increasingly powerful central body, the Trades Union Congress, itself the result of Trades Council initiatives.

Victorian cities struggled to create a civic consciousness through the formation of municipal councils, made possible by the 1835 Municipal Reform Act. If the municipal councils represented the urban middle-class factory owner and builder and the older professional classes, the trade councils, appearing in the 1860s, were the new forum for the organised working class, the skilled workers of the city, which provided a means of creating a consciousness of working-class unity. By the end of the 1860s trades councils had been established in all the major provincial towns, Birmingham, Sheffield, Edinburgh, Glasgow, Liverpool and Manchester among them.

The local impulse to the formation of what became a common pattern of alternative representation by men largely still unenfranchised was often the experience of industrial conflict which emphasised the need both for common action and for discussion. In London the builders' strike led directly to the setting up of the influential London Trades Council in 1860. George Odger of the Ladies' Shoemaker Society became secretary in 1862 and he gathered round him men like Robert Applegarth of the Carpenters and Daniel Guile of the Iron founders, and the support of such powerful trade union leaders increased in turn the authority and standing of the London Trades Council.

Local trade societies affiliated with the Council and by 1866 there were more than 100,000 affiliated members. Its policy has been summed up by its historian as 'caution, compromise, and, if possible, arbitration' (75). The LTC in its report of 1864 put itself solidly on the side of amalgamation and size: 'It is worthy of remark [so ran the report] that societies after they amalgamate, or otherwise become large, steer clearer of strikes and yet raise and sustain their wages much easier and with less expense than small societies have done, or we believe, ever will do.'

The Council's key role as a policy-maker had been achieved by controlling, through a system of credentials, the grant of money in industrial disputes such as that involving the London cigarmakers in 1863 or the London typefounders in 1865. Provincial societies sent delegations to the Bell Inn, Old Bailey, the LTC headquarters seeking advice and assistance. In the early 1860s, the London Trades Council had become briefly the leaders of British trade unionism, and their records show societies as industrially and geographically diverse as the Stourbridge Spademakers or the Birmingham Flint Glass Cutters making the same pilgrimage to the Bell.

In Birmingham the local trades council arose from a dispute which had much in common with the problems successfully faced by the engineers in the 1840s, the insistence by employers on the need for a Discharge Note, a compulsory reference that workers must have before re-employment. From the employers' viewpoint it can be seen as a safeguard against shiftless or drunken employees, an equivalent of the testimonial in domestic service – the good reference essential for re-employment. But issued without any safeguard for the employee it can clearly be an arbitrary way of victimising employees who are merely independent or who are particularly vociferous 'society' men.

In the Birmingham building trades the Discharge Note was first made compulsory for carpenters and joiners and resulted in a city-wide strike (84, 33). The men received conflicting advice from Applegarth of the ACSJ and a representative of General Union of Carpenters and Joiners in Manchester. London ordered them back and Manchester proposed that they should stay out until the employers made an official promise to abandon the note (they had already withdrawn it on the intervention of the Mayor of Birmingham). Only a joint arbitration committee under mayoral auspices finally resolved the dispute.

The carpenters' strike was one stimulus to the formation of a wider representative body in the city; the other was victimisation of a local trade unionist, a certain William Carroll. On behalf of his society, the Labourers' Society, William Carroll had given notice to his employer that society members could not work with 'non-society' men and then, as the employer stood firm, all members of the Labourers' Society gave notice. Subsequently, William Carroll was arrested and sentenced to six weeks imprisonment under the Master and Servant Act.

The initiative to set up a local trades council came from the building workers, who had twice been in confrontation with their employers.

Roger Bateson, then National Treasurer for the General Union of Carpenters and Joiners called a meeting at the Tamworth Arms, Moor Street, on 22 May, 1866. From this meeting came the Birmingham Trades Council, heavily representative of the traditional crafts: the carpenters, cabinet makers, wood turners, cordwainers and mill sawyers. Of the forty-three trade societies in the town only thirteen were founder members of a council which declared its objective as watching over 'the social and political rights of the workers and generally to further the benefits of Trade Unionism'.

THE 'JUNTA' AND POLITICAL INVOLVEMENT

By the 1860s Britain had firmly established her role as the leading industrial nation of the world. Her European neighbours looked with envy on her liberal institutions and admired her outspoken opposition to oppression abroad. Mid-Victorian liberalism, sharpened by English dissent, criticised Russian autocracy and the persecution of Italian liberals and nationalists. Middle-class liberal attitudes were also reflected in the London trade unions in the support given to Polish exiles, to Italian radicals such as Garibaldi and Mazzini, and to Lincoln's commitment to emancipation.

British trade unionism in the 1860s, despite what might to its historians seem its obvious legal and industrial disabilities, was the model of advanced working-class organisation compared with continental working-class institutions. Where in Europe trade union organisation was permitted overtly by law, its members were still hounded by the secret police, a situation which worsened with the growth of Bakuninist ideas with their emphasis on trade societies as agencies for revolution rather than betterment and improvement.

The leaders of that trade unionism were the organisers of the principal London trade unions, the men the Webbs have called the Junta, the five powerful general secretaries: Robert Applegarth of the Carpenters, William Allan of the Engineers, Daniel Guile of the Ironfounders, Edwin Coulson of the Bricklayers, George Odger of the Ladies' Shoemakers' Society. Between them they came to be seen as standing for the new type of trade unionists yet in the provinces George Potter and his newspaper the *Beehive* often wielded more influence; indeed in the 1860s the voice of the working-class seemed often to have the tones of Potter and the *Beehive*. Potter himself was a joiner and chairman of the Progressive Society of Carpenters and Joiners. He emerged into prominence as secretary of the London Building Trades Conference from 1859–61. A man of great natural gifts and overwhelming energy, during the strike and lockout he quickly came to appreciate the power of the press. *Reynold's' Newspaper,* one of the most important legacies from Chartism, was the only newspaper actively to support the building workers, although the *Morning Advertiser* gave full coverage to Potter and his strike committee.

Potter was a determined advocate but his commitment to the nine-hour movement led him to withdraw from the final negotiations, thereby missing the chance, as Stephen Coltham observes, 'of becoming the first secretary to the new union (the ASCJ). Furthermore despite his new prominence, he made no attempt to secure a place on the newly formed London Trades Council. Potter was to involve all his consider-able talents in managing and running the *Beehive* newspaper which became the voice of working class radicalism in the 1860s and continued to appear until 1878, for the last two years under the new name of *The Industrial Review.* The aim of the *Beehive* were trenchantly defined in the prospectus as concerned with 'the claims of the working classes for a complete reform in Parliament; in reduction in the present hours of Labour; the co-operative system (89).'

With aims such as these, of which the first looked back to Chartism, Potter understandably tangled with some of the members of the London Trades Council, such as William Allan, who were hostile to any political role for trade unions. But the confrontation with the Junta turned on two unrelated matters. The *Beehive* often stood for militant action, where Applegarth saw the strike as 'a double-edged weapon, to be used with great caution.' Again, Potter, through his columns, appealed to the wider audience of the provincial trade unions, and used with skill the natural dislike of the trade unionist outside the capital to the London Trades Council which so often, in their view acted as though they represented the whole of British trade unions. The public often took George Potter and the *Beehive* to be the true spokesman for the working classes, a position which Potter did nothing to disclaim. The rift between Potter and the Junta widened during the political reform agitation after the mid-60s when the Junta worked through its middle-class allies and the Reform League and Potter set up in opposition the London Working Men's Association aimed at reducing both the Reform League's influence and that of the Junta.

Of the five who comprised the Junta Robert Applegarth was perhaps the most outstanding, a high contributions, high benefits man, and anxious to replace industrial strife by industrial co-operation (112). His policy was directed to reducing and controlling strikes. In 1865 he persuaded his executive to resolve that 'under no circumstances will any branch be allowed to strike without first obtaining the sanction of this Council, whether it be for a new privilege or against an encroachment on existing ones'. To cool the striking temper further, he devised a strike application form which a branch had to complete when seeking authorisation for a strike. Conciliation and arbitration Applegarth considered to be the way forward for trade unions and management, and he was insistent that arbitration meant that both sides were bound by the decision.

Although Applegarth was the most forceful, and certainly the bluntest of the Junta, his approach was common to all five members, and George Odger, secretary of the London Trades Council for ten years after 1862, kept the Trades Council on the same lines.

As Marx observed the English trade unionists lacked 'the spirit of generalisation and revolutionary ardour' (62) but their cautious and moderate approach to industrial policy did not mean that the London leaders cut themselves off entirely from politics or shared the ASE opposition to political involvement. Applegarth, Odger (a gifted and persuasive speaker) and Potter shared a common stand on support for radical causes and for the extension of the franchise. There were many trade unionists who shared Mazzini's generous vision of a Europe based on rule by the people. Many, too, hoped that the trade union organisation evolved in Britain could be copied by their less fortunate brothers in Europe.

This political concern took many different forms. In 1862, for instance, the London Trades Council sent a fraternal address to the Naples Trades Council, with copies sent to the Garibaldi Italian Unity Committee, for Garibaldi ranked as one of the great folk heroes of English radicals. In the same year the London Trades Council created a committee in which both Applegarth and Potter were officials, concerned to establish a fund for Lancashire cotton workers made unemployed by the failure of American cotton supplies. This committee had both a political as well as a charitable purpose and the 'cottonocracy' in Lancashire and the 'slave dealers of the South' were jointly castigated (101).

For a short time it looked as if prosaic, pragmatic English trade unionists would be caught up in the whirlwind of European politics when in 1864 the International Working Men's Association was formed with Odger as president. This burgeoned into a wider body with a General Council, with Odger serving as chairman; support came later from Coulson, Howell and Applegarth. At the peak of its influence the International in England could only count on 50,000 affiliated members. Some apolitical trade unionists like William Allan refused any link with the International. What purpose did Odger and his friends see for it? At its first meeting Odger spoke and give an address to the Workmen of France (62), Mazzinian in its concern to weaken 'the power of the despots'. When he turned to trade union matters he made it abundantly clear that he was primarily concerned to prevent the import of blackleg labour.

The standing of English trade unions abroad was demonstrated at the time of the building lockout in Geneva in 1868, when the building workers appealed to the General Council in England and claimed that contact between 'English and European workers through the medium of the International had had the effect of accelerating the formation of trade unions on the continent and quickened their course of action' (62). If as Postgate (18) claims 'the intention of Applegarth was to extend the benefits of Trade Unionism to the Continent', this was clear evidence of success. However subsequently the gulf widened between English trade unionists and their counterparts in Europe, worsened by the ideological preoccupations of the Europeans displayed forcibly at the Congresses held in Geneva and Brussels in the late 1860s. In 1871 when Marx published his *Civil War in France*, English trade unionists drew back in alarm at being associated with the concept of a revolutionary and armed working class, and the shortlived alliance foundered. The struggle between Marx and Bakunin had no relevance to English trade union politics, dominated as they then were with the legal results of the Royal Commission of 1867 and the political consequences of the 1867 Reform Act.

English trade unionists had worked alongside middle-class radicals for Garibaldi and for Polish independence and that interclass alliance reappeared again in 1865 with the Reform League [doc. 9]. Supported by the Liberal barrister Edmond Beales as President and with widely based working-class support — Potter, Odger, Howell, Applegarth — the League campaigned in the 1865 General Election for middle-class radical candidates, including John Stuart Mill at Westminster and Thomas Hughes at Lambeth.

George Howell's biographer (11) claims that 'the agitation helped to set the context' within which the 1867 Reform Act was passed and 'That it is doubtful that parliamentary opinion would have accepted reform as inevitable without popular pressure'. Certainly the League under Howell's guidance helped to cement the Lib-Lab pact which was to underpin labour politics down to the end of the century. Both in the implicit Lib-Lab alliance which presented evidence to the Commision of Inquiry, and in the new potentialities revealed by the Reform Act, the shape of the future was emerging: collaboration with middle-class Liberals to secure improvements — assimilation, the blurring of class divisions rather than politicisation and the class isolation which the International had seen as the necessary goal of working-class organisation.

With a Reform Act on the statute book which went a good way to securing universal male suffrage in the towns, the League's usefulness was over. In 1869 it was replaced by the Labour Representation League, supported by Allan, Applegarth, Howell and Odger and committed to securing the return to the Commons of 'qualified working men'.

LABOUR LEGISLATION AND NEW INSTITUTIONS

Trade Union Act 1871

The Reform Act of 1867 altered the balance of the voting forces in the towns, a fact quickly recognised by Joseph Chamberlain in Birmingham (77) who immediately mobilised working-class voters in a new-style Liberal party. For organised trade unionists there was at last the implicit promise of political power, a bright hope partly dimmed by two unrelated threats to their position offered by the Sheffield outrages in 1866 and the Hornby v. Close Judgment in 1867.

Of these two threats, the Sheffield outrages were the more alarming, overturning as it seemed the hard-won respectability of Victorian trade unionism, with the press filled with stories of gunpowder plots, and attacks on uncooperative workmen directly implicating the secretary of a Sheffield grinders' union. Industrial Sheffield was dominated by small firms in which the workforce was organised by small and narrow local unions which had traditionally found it difficult to establish effective trade union control of local craftsmen. As a result rather unorthodox methods of discipline had for some time been imposed, of which the least oppressive was 'rattening', the removal of a workman's tools. Robert Applegarth was prepared to defend the practice of 'sending members to Coventry' and could see a case for 'rattening' even though he personally disapproved of it. The discipline used against recalcitrant trade unionists had culminated in gunpowder attacks, the murder of a sawgrinder in 1859 and the death of an innocent householder in 1866 when a grinder's house had been blown up.

The outrages stirred deepseated middle-class fears and suspicions of the habits and practices of trade unions and raised fundamental problems about the extent to which coercion could rightfully be used by trade unionists against defaulting members. Henry Cutts, the Sheffield filesmiths' secretary, put the argument in this way: 'If a member refuses to pay his proportion towards the protection (of his labour) equally with others ... a certain amount of force may be necessary to make him comply in a reasonable manner.' The debate began to move on to familiar ground when trade unionists questioned how far men who entered a trade ought to join the trade society, for otherwise they would be receiving benefits and wages won by the action of a union to which they did not belong. Was joining a trade union an obligation which workmen must be brought to accept, if necessary by the judicious use of pressure?

While Sheffield was blurring the national image of trade unions, the Hornby *v* Close judgment administered yet another blow to the standing of British unions. The Friendly Societies' Act (1855) was thought to have given legal cover to trade union funds and their legal position had been further strengthened by the Molestation of Workmen Act (1859) which excluded peaceful picketing from legal penalties. The Court of Queen's Bench, headed by the Lord Chief Justice, held when the Boilermakers' Society tried to recover £24 from their Bradford secretary, that as a trade union the Society did not come within the Friendly Societies Act and furthermore that the Society was 'in restraint of trade' and therefore illegal.

The whole new respectability of trade unions was now destroyed. Not only were their now considerable funds at risk but their institutional role, with their rules, regulations, formal meetings and paid secretaries, was now firmly excluded from the new industrial life of the country, and seemingly they were back to their position before the repeal of the Combination Laws.

The Disraeli government set up a Royal Commission of Inquiry, prompted by Robert Applegarth who had no wish to see the general practice and procedures confused with the unlawful behaviour of the notorious Sheffield societies. The Inquiry was given terms of reference covering the whole area of trade unionism, and the London Trades Council and the Junta sought the help of their middle-class allies, in particular Frederic Harrison and Thomas Hughes, both of whom were appointed to the Commission. Indeed it is arguable that this is really the time in which the term 'Junta' rightly describes the five London trade union leaders who now began to meet secretly to work out a joint policy to present to the Royal Commission.

The Junta's efforts did not go unchallenged for a rival provincial group led by George Potter also sought to influence the Royal Commission. Through the agency of the London Working Men's Association, Potter called together a national Trade Union Conference with a claimed membership of 200,000 trade unionists — miners, boilermakers, stonemasons and iron and steel workers. Potter's nominee, Thomas

Connolly, the conference chairman was proposed as a trade union representative for the Commission.

On their side, the Junta had established the Conference of Amalgamated Trades to present their case, and Robert Applegarth was appointed their spokesman. With their Liberal allies on the Commission, Harrison and Hughes, Junta strategy was to show the Commission the acceptable face of trade unionism. When Thomas Connolly was excluded from the meetings of the Commission after a tactless speech, Robert Applegarth and his friends made no attempt to save him. Both Applegarth and Allan sought to impress on the Commission that the trade unions were 'primarily national friendly societies' as the Webbs later called them. They were not interested in strikes, in restriction on the number of apprentices, or preventing the use of new machinery. Their main concerns were the standard rate and the standard hours. In his evidence, Applegarth summarised the objects of his own association, the Amalgamated Society of Carpenters and Joiners [doc. 10] :

The object of this society is to raise funds for the mutual support of its members in case of sickness, accident, superannuation, for the burial of members and their wives, emigration, loss of tools, by fire, water and theft, and for assistance to members out of work; also for granting assistance in cases of extreme distress not otherwise provided for by the rules.

Strikes, picketing, driving hard bargains with employers, all seemd a long way from objectives such as these. The Junta's deliberate playing down of the industrial purposes of trade unions made logical the Liberal government's refusal to include peaceful picketing in the new Trade Union Bill of 1871 which resulted from the work of the Commissioners.

The skill with which the Junta presented their case was reflected in the approval of *The Times* in which a leading article on 8 July 1869 advised 'True statemanship will seek neither to augment nor to reduce their influence, but, accepting it as a fact, will give it free scope for legitimate development.' The Royal Commission agreed largely with *The Times*. Both the majority and the minority report recommended that the trade unions were legalised. Where the Commissioners differed was on the restrictions which should be imposed on the unions. The majority report proposed protection of funds to those unions who were free from such restrictive practices as limiting the number of apprentices or limiting the use of machinery and others of a similar kind [doc. 11]. The minority were for protection without any limitation being placed on the codes under which trade unions operated.

With the fall of the Disraeli government in 1868, Gladstone took over but the Liberals initially were reluctant to carry through the recommendations of the Royal Commission. However Mundella and Hughes, two Liberal supporters, introduced into the House a Bill drafted by Harrison which was based upon the minority report. A meeting of trade unionists at Exeter Hall heard Mundella and Hughes promise that they would force the government to show its hand by a vote on the Bill. Finally the Liberals government gave way and promised to introduce their own Bill. This finally reached the House in 1871 and embodied all the recommendations of the minority members of the Commission. However it went further along the logical line the Junta had claimed they had been following and banned all forms of picketing. The only concession to trade union pressure the Liberal government made was to separate the picketing clauses from the main trade union Bill and incorporate them in a separate Act, the Criminal Law Amendment Act. Trade unions were now legalised but picketing, the one activity considered by union members as fundamental to successful strike action, was denied to them. That the danger was real was soon made clear. In different parts of the country judges passed short sentences for picketing offences. In London a general strike of gas stokers produced sentences ranging from six weeks to twelve months. The new respectability had proved wafer thin and for men on strike there was now the real and constant danger of prison. The dark days of the early nineteenth century seemed to have returned.

The Trades Union Congress

It was Potter who saw that the strength of provincial trade unionism ought to be made use of in trade union affairs and he threw his considerable weight behind the initiative from the Wolverhampton Trades Council calling for a more general framework for the trade union movement. Individual unions or individual trades councils would not defeat employers but a combination of both in a national body could fight more effectively. The resolution passed by the Wolverhampton Trades Council said boldly that 'the time has arrived when the trades of the United Kingdom ought to take action conjointly to rebut the lockout system now so prevalent with the capitalists.' On the basis of this resolution Potter developed the idea of district Labour Parliaments meeting quarterly and a national Labour Parliament meeting once a year (34).

The London Trades Council was unenthusiastic but support for Potter's proposal came from the provinces. In Sheffield the Sheffield

Association of Organised Trades called a conference attended by 138 delegates with 280,000 workers behind them. This meeting burgeoned forth into the United Kingdom Alliance of Organised Trades with plans for an annual conference. Although the new Sheffield-based confederation received its death blow from the revelation that its treasurer, Broadhead, was involved in the outrages, nevertheless a modest precedent had been established for a provincial initiative in calling a national conference (32).

In 1867 two events worked together to give greater urgency to the need for a national representative body – the Royal Commission on Trade Unions and the implicit promise of the Reform Act of 1867 that working men could now use their vote to return working men to Parliament. No party could now ignore the new voter, nor for that matter could the Royal Commission ignore the new political situation created by Disraeli's Act. Potter and the provinces saw this as the moment in which to exploit their new political power. The Junta, however, preferred to wait on the publication of the Royal Commission's report.

Already in March 1867 Potter, Alexander Macdonald and the provincial trades councils had challenged the hegemony of the Junta by the calling of the Conference of Trades at St Martin's Hall, London, and the subsequent appointment of their chairman, Thomas Connolly, to represent their interests at the meetings of the Royal Commission. Once again Potter seized the initiative in alliance with the provinces when on 2 June 1868 the Manchester and Salford Trades Council summoned a conference in Manchester.

The original purpose of this meeting was not to create a political pressure group or even to create a general council with increased bargaining power. The final push which brought the TUC into existence came from William Dronfield, a compositor, who had given a paper to the Social Science Association which they had failed to publish. Dronfield proposed that trade societies should hold congresses of their own, modelled to a great extent on the Social Science Association, and the Manchester and Salford Trades Council had taken up the idea and then sent out invitations to trade councils and also to individual unions. Before the meeting the topics for debate were listed and papers solicited from representatives.

The first Trades Union Congress had thirty-four delegates, representing 118,000 members. There were some notable absentees: neither London nor Glasgow Trades Council sent representatives. No one came from the Junta. Only George Potter and John Kane (of the Ironworkers) had any national reputation. They debated a whole range of topics: the need for trade unions, the length of the working day, technical education, arbitration, the law and trade unions. In all the proceedings lasted a week.

In a famous resolution the Congress expressed its wish to meet every year. 'It is', said Congress, 'highly desirable that the trades of the United Kingdom should hold an annual congress for the purpose of bringing the trades into closer alliance, and to take action in all parliamentary matters pertaining to the general interests of the working class' (35).

The second TUC met in August 1869 at the Oddfellows Hall, Temple Street, Birmingham, where the main item for discussion was the report of the Royal Commission and the form legislation should take. One representative, A.W. Walton, secretary of a Co-operative Building Society, read a paper in which he argued for the creation of a party for working men. Working men, he said 'should unite, form a working man's party and at future elections where two Liberal candidates had to be elected they should insist on nominating one, allowing the middle class to choose the other'. This proposal seems to suggest a working man's party which would work with the Liberals rather than work entirely independently. The resolution was adopted, but the TUC were slow to take the first steps to secure a representation of working men's interests in the House.

Whereas Walton's resolution envisaged working men in Parliament representing working men's interests, another TUC resolution promised support for the Labour Representation League which had William Allan as treasurer and a barrister as president and was concerned to 'secure the return to Parliament of qualified working men ... [and] where deemed necessary, recommend and support as candidates from the other classes such persons as have studied the great Labour problems and have proved themselves friendly to an equitable settlement'. This was a far less radical proposal and was widely supported both by Potter and leaders of the Junta.

Before the second TUC dispersed, Congress decided that the London Trades Council should have responsibility for organising the next meeting. Allan and Applegarth, and the rest of the London leadership, resented the emergence of the TUC and faced the criticisms of provincial trade unionists who saw London as uncaring of the interests of smaller, less influential, provincial societies. There was a fundamentally different approach which divided London from the provinces, for the Junta were opposed to any legislation which would distinguish working men from the rest of society. In their view the artisan was socially equal to the middle class and nothing must be done which would undermine that assumption. B.C. Roberts (34) shows that 'the London Trades Council . . . was pushed into summoning Congress in 1871 because of the insistent demands that were coming from the provincial trades councils'. Finally Congress met in March 1871 in the Portland Rooms, off Tottenham Court Road, with in all fifty-seven delegates from forty-nine different societies with a total membership of 300,000.

Congress met each year after that and in 1875 actually met twice, once at Liverpool and the second time at Glasgow. Trade union influence and power were shown rather differently in the 1874 elections when the Labour Representation League supported thirteen trade union candidates. Among them were George Odger, George Howell, Henry Broadhurst, Alexander Macdonald and two other members of the Parliamentary Committee. Only Macdonald and Thomas Burt of the Northumberland Miners were elected, but this electoral success marks the beginning of a new and potentially extremely significant phase in trade union history. The TUC was now established and had helped to achieve a new legal status for trade unions, a success which paradoxically had led many unionists to think that the TUC and its Parliamentary Committee had now completed their useful life.

The TUC Parliamentary Committee

The first TUC had modelled itself very closely on the National Association for the Promotion of Social Science. It was essentially a learned body, presenting papers and exchanging views about common problems. Its role was to be quite distinct from that of pressure group, a role reserved for the London Trades Council and its elder statesmen. The relative failure of the LTC to secure full trade union rights, a failure which became markedly clear as the Trade Union Bill went steadily through Parliament, altered the original nature of the TUC and permanently reduced the standing and influence of the London Trades Council.

The London Trades Council had been assigned the responsibility of calling the third TUC but dragged its collective feet. When the TUC finally met (in March 1871) the Liberal Bill was well on the way to becoming law and Congress turned its mind to the new problems the unions were facing and elected a new body, the Parliamentary Committee, the forerunner of the General Council 'to watch over the passage of the Trade Union Bill'. Its original brief required the Committee to cooperate with the London Trades Council and its original members included not only Potter but Lloyd Jones, a contributor to the *Beehive*, together with the powerful Alexander Macdonald, the Scottish miners' leader, and George Howell.

Macdonald had recently been involved in the campaign to reform the law of contract as it affected contracts between employer and workman. This law had been a source of bitter grievance. If an employer broke his contract with his men, he could be sued for damages and required to pay what he owed. For a workman the law worked very differently. If he was absent, or if he left his job, this ranked as a criminal offence for which the law provided no other penalty but prison. An employer could give evidence against a worker and defend himself, but a worker could not give evidence against an employer and defend himself. In the 1860s there were more than 10,000 such cases a year and 1,558 workmen had been sent to prison in 1865 for offences under this law. The indignities visited on the unhappy man were many. He might be taken from his own house, set before a magistrate (often himself an employer) with sometimes the trial even taking place in the magistrate's private house. As a member of the London Trades Council had said this was 'justice's justice'. Since an amending Act of 1848 this aspect of the procedure had been largely abandoned in England. In Scotland there had been no change and indeed the offending workman was usually arrested. The Master and Servant Law, by which an employer could coerce workers back to work by the threat of prosecution, added to the armoury of employers' weapons in a strike.

The Glasgow Trades Council in the 1860s campaigned strenuously for reform in this law. In 1863 the Council, and in particular Alexander Campbell and George Newton, with the support of Alexander Macdonald, set out to reform the law. A London conference was called (in 1864) to discuss the workings of the law, which appointed an executive committee, virtually the Glasgow Trades Council in another guise. The Junta and George Potter supported the campaign and in 1867 the new Master and Servant Act replaced the iniquities of the old system. It was still open for employers to bring a criminal charge against a worker and only the Employers' and Workmen's Act (1875) ended the social and legal distinctions traditional in the industrial relations between master and man.

There was, perhaps, no such comparable injustice in the 1871 Trade Union Act. The new law gave much needed protection to trade union funds and allowed unions to register as Friendly Societies under the 1855 Friendly Societies Act. Furthermore the Act laid down that trade unions were not held in law as in restraint of trade and therefore could not be charged under the common law. The corollary to the 1871 Act, the Criminal Law Amendment Act, forbade such acts as 'molestation and obstruction' 'with a view to coerce' an employer.

The danger lay in the interpretation of 'coerce'. How far would this apply to strikes and to picketing?

That the danger was real was soon made explicit, in the way in which the judiciary interpreted the Act, with five London gas stokers sent down for a year in 1872 and in the following year the turbulent wives of Chipping Norton farm labourers sentenced for the crime of hooting at blacklegs. The new Parliamentary Committee moved into action and campaigned publicly against the Act. They submitted evidence to their friends in Parliament, Mundella and Hughes in particular, to persuade the Liberal Government to amend its own statute.

A change in the law had, however, to wait upon a change in government. Gladstone's government had shown the limitations of 'Lib-Lab' cooperation and had underlined the Liberal elite's determination to preserve the industrial status quo. Disraeli and the new Tory administration, committed ideologically to Tory democracy and politically to recruiting the new 1867 voter, introduced a new Bill, which became the Conspiracy and Protection of Property Act (1875). This gave the trade unions all they wanted. No act committed in combination was criminal unless the same act was criminal if committed individually, and peaceful picketing was legalised.

These labour laws of 1867 and 1871 and the two Tory enactments of 1875 gave trade unions a recognised part in the structure of British industry. Their friendly society activities, so heavily stressed before the Royal Commission, were now protected: their right to strike, to picket, and to persuade non-strikers peacefully was guaranteed by law. Until trade union objectives were once more to be altered by the changed conditions of the 1890s and by the Taff Vale decision, the essentially liberal concept of free collective bargaining had been confirmed by Parliament.

Conciliation Boards

If the 1875 legislation might suggest that trade unions had become part of the established code of practice in British industry – a view which could hardly be supported by the continuing struggle in many industries such as the railways to secure recognition – the process of acceptance had gone much further in five industries where conciliation and arbitration procedures were firmly established. These were the Nottinghamshire hosiery industry, the North of England iron industry, boot and shoe manufacture and cotton spinning and in mining, where there were extensive sliding-scale agreements. These techniques developed rapidly after the 1860s and were widely accepted when new agreements produced without major conflict gave increased awards, but in the bad years after 1873 when, as Philip S. Bagwell points out (58), only nine of sixty-one decisions brought wage improvements, they were viewed with increasing suspicion.

Technological improvement, increased productivity and rising markets contributed to the developments of joint boards. Before Mundella set up his Hosiery Board in 1860, J.R. Hicks (102) has shown that there had been two earlier shortlived attempts, in the silkweaving trade in Macclesfield, where a joint board set up in 1849 had survived for four years, and on the Wear, where the shipwrights and masters worked together from 1850 to 1852. In Nottingham the hosiery industry was facing its fourth strike in a year when A.J. Mundella suggested a conference of employers and men, from which the Nottingham Hosiery Board developed as an effective form of conciliation within the industry.

V.L. Allen (106) makes the point that 'the National Association for the Promotion of Social Science became the forum for the advocates of conciliation and arbitration after its formation in 1857.' Certainly machinery of this kind seemed to accord with one strand in Liberal ideology, to offer workers a share in that expansion and enrichment which mid-Victorian England was securing for its capitalist entrepreneur.

Mundella was to form part of that select band of arbitrators and conciliators (Judge Rupert Kettle, Thomas Hughes, Q.C. were others) whose services were increasingly in demand by those employers who came to share the social and economic philosophy of industrial partnership. The strength of trade union support was shown at the meeting of the United Kingdom Alliance of Organised Trades in Sheffield in 1866, the forerunner of the TUC, where trade union speakers urged the establishment of conciliation and arbitration councils.

David Dale, the Quaker ironmaster, who set up the Conciliation Board for the Manufactured Iron Trade of the North of England, has described how he was personally influenced by Mundella's success (107). His achievement was in what might have seemed a peculiarly intractable industry, expanding very rapidly but with a new and undisciplined labour force, unknown to each others and strangers to the locality. There had been a wave of strikes and the ironmasters, with a long order book, had sunk a great deal of capital in the industry. Dale suggested that some of the workers' leaders should go to Nottingham at his expense and look at the working of Mundella's scheme. They went and returned asking for 'a Board of Arbitration constituted and arranged as Mr Mundella's scheme, (103). The conciliation Board which resulted from this move in 1869 became a model for others. Dale was fortunate in his counterpart on the men's side, John Kane, President of the Association of Ironworkers, who became the men's secretary to the Conciliation Board. Dale encouraged other ironmasters to recognize the union and by 1873 Kane's union had grown to a membership of 35,000. By 1879, however, membership had sunk to 1,400 and from then on there was a slow rise to 10,000 by 1892. V.L. Allen comments (106) that 'the introduction of sliding scale agreements was one of the factors which cause the membership of the association of Ironworkers to decline' and more generally, 'where conciliation and arbitration were employed and succeded by sliding-scale agreements, trade unionism was contained and disarmed at a significant stage of its growth'.

It might equally be argued that Kane's willingness to work the system was a realistic recognition of the economic position of the industry, worthy of a contemporary moderate trade union general secretary. Indeed Clegg, Fox and Thompson comment that 'sliding-scale agreements show a realisation that automatic adjustments through the formal machinery of the board were to be preferred to the frontal clashes which had destroyed so many unions in the two [iron and coal] industries' (36)'

The new initiatives developed in industry were taken up in Parliament by Lord St Leonards in 1867, when he tried to extend the practice and make provision for joint boards, a statute which was never used. Mundella himself in 1872, by the statute which bears his name, tried to encourage the use of arbitration and to give it the protection of law.

Conciliation machinery, while reducing the employers' prerogatives, also diminished the right of a workman to withhold his labour to secure advancement of his claim. It established itself in expanding or new industries, but not in industries where craft unions were strongly entrenched. 'Through much of the nineteenth century custom was the most important authority in British industrial relations' (Clegg, (36). Trade unions were traditionally concerned to resist changes in customary practice in industry. The Operative Buildiers' Union (1831-33) was created to oppose the new system of general contracting in which a master builder would offer an estimate for a completed building, thereby invading the traditional prerogatives of craftsmen to offer separate contracts for each separate craft operation involved in the finished building.

Customs were increasingly formalised into trade union decisions which established rates of pay and hours of work. Craft unions seeking to improve rates of pay sought to negotiate with employers, and this became the practice of 'collective bargaining'. From bargaining over rates of pay the next step was by way of agreements over overtime and

53

shiftwork, but some areas such as the parctice governing recruitment of apprentices was still left to custom. 'Collective bargaining' was sacrosanct and fundamentally local, with district rates which employers within the area could not undercut unless they employed non-union men, a practice which would lead to the withdrawal of all union men from their site.

Conciliation differed from collective bargaining in that it implied a willingness to reach a compromise without confrontation, and furthermore the settlement could have implications for differentials within an industry which by custom were left to the collective bargaining of the trade unions. If as was normal only the selling price governed the movement of wages, what would happen when prices fell, even though profits remained constant, because of a reduction in the costs of the operation? Was there not a clear danger that trade unions would cease to represent the interests of their members and be caught up in an agreement machinery concerned entirely with employers interests?

Conciliation boards would normally be made up of an equal number of workers and employers, with workers usually chosen by the unions involved. The chairman might himself be an independent, in which case he would often be called in to act as an umpire, or if the chairman arose from the meeting, there might be provision for calling in an outsider chosen in an agreed way to pronounce on particular issues (94).

It was a short step from this to the attempt to end industrial strife by arbitration, and boards often tried to secure an end to a dispute amongst themselves by the use of arbitration procedure. For the state to set up arbitral machinery was a logical extension of this practice so that all British industry might be able to draw up arbitration procedures to end disputes and end stoppages. The major move forward came from the report of the Royal Commission on Labour, 1891-94, one of whose recommendations formed the basis of the Conciliation Act 1896. The Royal Commission looked for a more rational way of settling industrial disputes than strike and lockout and considered the possibility of state intervention; however their final recommendation favoured 'the moral sanction'. The Conciliation Act repealed all previous legislation concerning conciliation and arbitration and gave the Board of Trade power to appoint an arbitrator, if asked to do so by both sides to an industrial dispute. Conciliation boards were asked to register with the Board of Trade, and employers' reluctance to bring the state into their affairs is evidenced by the number of boards who had actually registered by the eve of the First World War, 19 out of 325 (58). The Conciliation Act may be seen as the tentative framework of what has become an extensive state service and much of its success in the early years depended upon the style, integrity and ability of the government conciliator, G.R. Askwith.

The sliding scale

In mining, the counterpart of the hosiery industry's Joint Board, was the development of the sliding scale. Both depended on the tacit assumption of a doctrine of common interest within the industry and in mining – except in Scotland where mineowners were traditionally hostile to unions – trade union strength permitted the establishment of joint committees to determine wages. In Northumberland, Yorkshire and Durham, such joint committees were well established. The mine owners argued that wages should be linked to the selling price of coal, with all that involved in terms of differing outlets for different districts, and trade unionists were subscribing openly to the view that 'prices should rule wages'.

The logic of this attitude if the worker accepted the *laissez faire* doctrine that his wage depended upon his worth in the market was irrefutable. In an open market prices must and do fluctuate; fluctuating prices must imply fluctuating profits and from the standpoint of the employer in a falling market there must always be a pressure to bring down costs. Some costs are irreducible but wages are not, unless one assumes a humane point beyond which wages cannot be reduced without danger to the health of the wage earner and his family.

In mining a sliding scale of wages had developed to take account of market changes. In coal mining, South Wales and Northumberland both had wages based upon the sliding scale. It was in many ways a refined device, for the actual basic rate was related to the nature of the seam and difficulty of working, and the actual pay was the basic rate varied by an amount fixed according to the price of coal.

The Webbs were extremely critical of union acceptance of the sliding scale and described the process as one in which 'the men gained their point at the cost of adopting the intellectual position of their opponents'. In one roundly condemnatory judgment, the Webbs proclaim: 'We see the sturdy leaders of many Trade Union battles gradually and insensibly accepting the capitalists axiom that wages must necessarily fluctuate according to the capitalists' profits, and even with the variation of market prices.' The Webbs accused trade unionists of abandoning their long defence of the standard of living and replacing it by 'faith in a scale of wages sliding up and down according to the commercial speculations of the controllers of the market'. V.L. Allen carries the attack even further **(106)** and argues that 'the consequence for trade unionism was that trade unions became or so it seemed at the time, largely unnecessary.' Clegg Fox and Thompson are critical of the Webbs' view and suggest that if union leaders in the seventies had not accepted the wage price link there would have been no unions of any strength in the industries concerned (36).

The doctrine that prices should rule wages could be demonstrated as beneficial in the 1870s when a Northumberland miner earned 9s 1½d a day and the wages of a skilled engine-driver at the top of his career grade was 45 shillings a week. It was less obvious by 1880 when the same miner's day rate had fallen to 4s 4d a day. The comfortable assumption of an identity of interest between labour and capital could not withstand the strain of the deteriorating conditions of life for the miner and his family.

The miners pressed two proposals on the owners: restriction of output so that the selling price would be maintained by control of production and a reduction of working hours to seven. This again the miners saw as an effective way of reducing output and avoiding a glut of coal on the market, with its consequent disastrous fall in prices.

Towards the end of the 1880s, miners' unions began to press for wage increases and from this union pressure sprang the Miners' Federation, set up in 1889 at Newport, largely the work of Ben Pickard, the tough Yorkshire mine leader, and Thomas Ashton from Lancashire, who became secretary. The Federation was committed to a firm policy of collective wage increases and to the eight-hour day. The Federation, which had nearly 100,000 members in 1889, went on to be one of the giant unions of Europe. It covered the whole of England and Scotland, except South Wales, still committed to the sliding scale, Northumberland and Durham, where the most developed forms of collective bargaining existed, and Fife and South Staffordshire.

The Federation set itself against the sliding scale wherever it continued to exist. What was so bitterly resented was the depth to which wages could fall when the mining industry hit a particularly bad patch. Two views began to gain ground: that the industry must have a minimum wage below which wages should never be permitted to fall, a minimum which was sufficient to maintain the miner and his family, and as a corollary of this, that an industry which made large profits in the good times should use some of that fat to support its workforce during a time of falling prices. Furthermore the central importance of coal to the nation, demonstrated so dramatically by Gladstone's intervention in the mining dispute of 1893, was coming to be understood by the miners. The economic importance of the home market was to strengthen the hand of the MFGB in their argument that together with the eight-hour day the abolition of the sliding scale must be their main objective.

5 New Growth: Railwaymen and Agricultural Workers

The Reform Acts of 1867 and 1884 had shifted the whole political balance in the constitution; political power now depended on the majority of the population, the working-class voter. The 1875 reforms in trade union law had freed the organised worker from any further attacks on his carefully forged and nurtured institutions. And yet neither change, politically or legally, produced any marked change in working-class political or industrial organisation. Politically, trade unionists generally taught their members to look to the Liberal party and to reforms which were significantly middle-class – even Joseph Chamberlain's 'Unauthorised Programme of 1885' with its bid for party leadership offered little to the working-class voter but more to the nonconformists, the Welsh or Scottish nationalist. By 1885 clearly the working-class was not sufficiently separately identifiable as to be worth a notice by a politician with a highly attuned ear for political potentialities. Industrially there had been no rapid expansion of trade union membership. It might almost seem as if the unions had reached their peak.

To G.D.H. Cole **(81)** the explanation for this failure to 'take off' lay in the Great Depression, which beginning after 1873, ended any real possibility of further expansion. An explanation which looks more to social than economic history is offered by H.A. Turner **(19)**. He advances the distinction between two types of unionism, open and closed, and uses the cotton industry to exemplify his thesis. Spinning typifies the closed society with a tight control of entry and restriction on the number of apprentices. While spinners behaved like a traditional craft society, which in essence they were, weavers, where no similar work group existed with one well-paid leader hedged around by 'hands', were an open society anxious to recruit all weavers in local associations, prepared as early as 1887 even to bring in 'reelers', a group less well skilled than themselves. Turner's argument is that in industry at large no major expansion took place because most unions were closed societies, jealously protecting their hardwon privileges within the uncertainties of a capitalist society.

Certainly this concern for what the Webbs called the 'method of mutual assurance' was to undergo considerable strain in the 1870s and 1880s, when society men were to find themselves hit by unemployment and short-time working, and socialist emphasis on the common struggle of the working class was to make headway even in the most tightly knit work groups. In the early 1870s, however, two new unions, a closed society of railwayworkers (or more accurately, semi-closed, for railmen had no control over entry) and an open society of agricultural workers were organised. They were established in radically different ways; the rail union was 'fostered'; the landworkers union sprang from what has been called 'a revolt of the fields'.

The railwaymen were taking no revolutionary step when they formed in 1871 the Amalgamated Society of Railway Servants under middle-class patronage. Indeed one of the objects of the union was 'to prevent strikes', an implicit comment on the timorous attitude of a union which stressed the need to promote 'a good and fair understanding between employers and employed'.

To be a railwayman, to wear the livery of one of the great companies was a matter of pride. Railwaymen regarded themselves as a cut above their ordinary working-class brothers. They had good reason to do so for in most ways they represented an aristocracy of labour, superior to the traditional aristocracy of the skilled worker. They were comparatively well paid and even the porter earned twice as much as an agricultural worker. They had security of tenure provided they were not guilty of insubordination or misconduct, although discipline on the railways was extremely strict. There were chances of rapid promotion during the great period of expansion from 1847 to 1873 when the work force rose from 47,000 to 274,000. Railwaymen could also expect yearly bonuses, railway cottages and membership of railway Friendly Societies, which offered sickness and accident benefit, and sometimes a retirement pension. The policy of the companies was to build up a loyal workforce in which obedience provided benefits in terms of promotions and perquisites and where the security of tenure railway employment offered would bind their workmen to the company (14, 24).

For well over thirty years railway companies had been remarkably successful in creating corporate loyalty for apart from local strikes the railways had had no major industrial dispute. In 1866 this corporate loyalty cracked when a major financial crisis made the companies look for economies, often by long unpaid overtime for all grades, drivers, firemen and guards. Protests and strikes were devastatingly defeated, followed usually by dismissal for the strikers [doc. 12].

Work in the mines, as on the railways, carries risks to life and limb. Yet mining trade unionism was not to benefit as railway trade unionism did from the groundswell of public interest in the plight of the overworked railwayman. The difference lies in the nature of the service: the railways provided a service industry in which the errors of its servants could imperil the lives of the public, its passengers, therefore it was in the public interest that railwaymen in key jobs, on the footplate or in signal boxes should not work up to nineteen hours a day and become so overtired that they could not function efficiently within the railway system. Railway technology by the 1860s was extremely advanced, judged by safety of track, bridges, embankments, rolling stock and power, but at a primitive level, judged in terms of the human servants of the machine.

The dangers of this situation had been brought home by the heavy accident rate on the railways, by articles in *The Telegraph* and *The Times*, by articles in the medical press which stressed that the *average* daily labour was just as important as the amount of labour on any one day and that as a consequence responsibility for rail accidents lay clearly with the railway companies. In the event, the prime mover, the founder, was not a railwayman or even a fellow trade unionist, but M.T. Bass, MP for Derby, a stockholder in the Midland Railway and as a brewer a major user of the railway system. It was he, well known as a local philanthropist, who had been approached by local railwaymen and who first raised, at a shareholders' meeting of the Midland, 'the excessive labour' of the pointsmen, guards and enginemen. The argument that began there continued in the House, and in the correspondence columns of *The Times* and led to Bass funding a journalist, James Greenwood of *The Telegraph*, to write articles on a railwayman's life which brought home to the public the dangers to travellers of a working week for a guard which might run from 90 hours and sometimes up to 120 hours. Bass went further in paying an ex-railway clerk, Charles Bassett Vincent, to tour the rail centres to create an opinion favourable to the setting up of a railway union.

In 1871, at a meeting held in London, the union was finally launched, fundamentally by Bass, although he was not at the meeting nor was he willing to become President. A well known Liberal, Dr J. Baxter Langley, took office as chairman. The union was an all-grades union, covering porters, clerks, the key footplate men and signal-box men. It had the initial advantage of public sympathy and support; it had the clear disadvantage of combining within one union men whose incomes and status were widely different and of being saddled with the doctrine that strikes were useless. As the union was not recognised by the rail companies, there were no established collective bargaining procedures. The contradictions of an all-purpose comprehensive, pacific union produced that 'spinelessness' that Normal McKillop describes (14).

The Amalgamated Society of Railway Servants concerned with

friendly society benefits and with lobbying Parliament for improvements, had a chequered and rather unsatisfactory early history. Its initial membership of 17,000 declined steadily but by 1888 had risen again to 15,000, not a remarkable success story from a potential membership of well over 200,000. By 1888 the union had modified its belief in the willingness of the rail companies to see reason. At the Annual General Meeting, held at Preston, when the dismissal of 189 railmen from the Midland after an unofficial strike was debated, the ASRS altered their rules to permit strike action with union support. For the first seventeen years of their existence the union had not sponsored a strike, and had worked on the assumption that arbitration would solve all grievances. The companies, however, had often shown themselves unwilling to go to arbitration and in this rule change the ASRS was moving towards the new aggressive form of trade unionism symbolised by, but predating, the 1889 London Dock Strike.

The same militancy was displayed in the independent railway union, the Associated Society of Locomotive Engineers and Firemen, which developed within the elite railway, the Great Western, in 1880. Rule 22 of the constitution laid down the conditions in which strike action could be taken and by which the union would provide strike pay. The ASLEF offered friendly society benefits too, but its proclaimed fundamental purpose was 'to advance the interests of its members' in their various professions and callings.

Railwaymen in their company houses, in their company livery, followed an almost military calling and their venture into unionisation might be seen as an attempt to convert theirs into a civilian calling. They did, however, live in towns, and within a working-class community extending beyond their own work into friendly societies and trade unions, traditions on which they could draw. The town with its factory, its pub, its chapel, offered meeting places and a training in political discipline. In the countryside nothing comparable existed, except the chapels from which so many of the leaders of the 'revolt of the fields' sprang. The politics of deference still commanded men's loyalties, there was no larger working-class community and even the publican might feel himself under threat from rural magistrates.

It is the more remarkable that trade unions once more, as in the mid-1830s, took root. From 1872 to 1874 the National Agricultural Labourers' Union organised agricultural workers in the South East, reaching the East Riding and East Anglia. At its peak the union had 150,000 members out of a work force of 650,000 and its most re-remarkable success was in 1872 when it secured wage increases up to 20 per cent for its members. It was finally defeated in 1874 by combinations of farmers who locked out their labourers and brought them to heel. Its expansion depended on several factors, not the least the relative shortage of labourers in some areas during these years. In particular the exceptional run of leaders, notably Joseph Arch, a self-employed worker and Primitive Methodist, a village craftsman with a range of skills running from hedging, ditching, ploughing to carpentry and building. It was he who, on the urgent prompting of local men, held that first historic meeting at Wellesbourne on 7 February 1872 from which this trade union of the fields grew. The Warwickshire labourers had the ready moral and financial support of Birmingham radicalism, and subscriptions came readily into their treasury from other unions and from sympathetic MPs. Arch's tone is caught in his speech at Derby in 1873 (9) when he called on agricultural labourers to demand the franchise and then as 'the wealth producing class they . . . could work for the good of the country and the community at large'.

Initially, agricultural trade unionism was a form of social protest from that rural class neglected by the Reform Act of 1867, stiffened as J. Dunbabin (85) has shown with nonconformist fervour and passion. 'It aimed', declared a leader, 'at raising them intellectually morally and politically.' A.J. Peacock (86) has collected evidence to show how deeply involved nonconformists were in Cambridgeshire and elsewhere in East Anglia where collections for the men were held in chapels. At the national level, the great Baptist preacher Charles Haddon Spurgeon gave his support in the disputes of 1874 and came to East Anglia to assert his sympathy.

Other forces were also at work – the ease of communications resulting from the growth of the railways in the 1860s meant that there could not only be ready connection between the local branches but also that news and newpapers, expressions of support, could easily reach the labourers. They were no longer the isolated community that they had been in the 1830s, and for a moment in the 1870s they were part of a working-class movement. Again literacy helped to spread the message and some villages such as Barford had the boon of a circulating library.

The movement in the countryside in the 1870s differed fundamentally from the labourers' revolts of the 1830s in that there was no use of force nor destruction of property. The weapon the men used was the new industrial weapon of the strike. Yet it cannot quite be seen as a precursor of the labourers' unions of the 1880s for it had a millenarianist flavour (85) which set it apart from those more pragmatic movements. There was a sense abroad that the 'day of redemption' was at hand, that forces outside human society were working for the liberation of the rural labourer. Nevertheless that did not preclude the provision of emigration schemes; nearly 700 men were moved out of East Anglia in 1874 and Arch claimed 200,000 labourers had been sent abroad by 1881. The praises of the colonies, notably New Zealand, were continually sung and the contrast made between the clodhoppers of England and the men of the new lands.

The farmers responded to the union by the formation of Defence Associations, on a county or district basis. In 1873, for instance, the Isle of Ely Defence Association was founded to fight the Peterborough Union in Haddenham and within a week had locked out 200 labourers. The farmers were determined to break the union and by June 1874 in East Anglia the union was financially unable to maintain the battle. That year proved to be crucial throughout the country and the union faded away rapidly, dwindling to a membership of 4,000 by 1889. After 1877 English agriculture faced the commercial challenge of prairie wheat and in the consequent depression of the rural areas emigration to the towns or overseas seemed the only means of self-improvement. The revolt of the 1870s produced several outstanding men such as Joseph Arch and Joseph Ashby of Tysoe (10) who challenged the tight control of rural England maintained by farmer and by squire. It provided heroes and martyrs for future movements and demonstrated that Hodge the clodhopper was as capable of collective and disciplined action as his counterpart in the towns (17).

6 'New Unionism'

The year 1889 has come to be seen as the springboard of 'the great leap forward', when trade unionism moved into those industrial employments such as those of gas workers and dockers where no trade unions previously existed and unskilled workers – labourers, not craftsmen – were brought the benefits of trade union membership. The traditional conservative-minded trade societies found themselves faced with militant trade unions, led often by socialists, prepared to carry through effective strike action in pursuit of the interests of their newly unionised members. The dock strike was seen as a symbol of the new forces at work and a pointer to the future.

Ben Tillett's epic struggle on behalf of the 'downtrodden' ranks with the Tolpuddle Martyrs and the general strike as one of the great events of trade union history, yet it must be seen within the context of the many changes which were taking place in English society and which in turn were affecting working men, whether trade unionists or not. Politically the working class now had within their grasp the chance to change the balance of forces and the political parties of late Victorian England were beginning to build into their programmes some promises of improvement. The Great Depression of the previous decade had left its mark even on the well-established craft societies, and trade unionists were concerned to find political means to prevent a recurrence of the high levels of unemployment of those years. The mid-Victorian liberal ethos which emphasised self-help was being challenged by Chamberlain's radicalism and philosophically by Oxford's T.H. Green with his emphasis on the use of the power of the state to promote the good life. The old comfortable assumptions about the nature of Victorian life were being eroded by the accumulating evidence of the extent of poverty and misery, and not only socialists were advocating collectivism and state intervention as a way of removing the worst injustices. Birmingham's 'gas and water socialism' in the 1870s and Disraeli's Public Health Act of 1875 were indications of the new mood of the times.

How far did socialist ideas affect the unions which appeared in the 1880s? Certainly both Will Thorne of the Gasworkers, and Tom Mann, President of the Dockers' Union, were Social Democratic Federation members and in both these strikes in 1889 middle-class socialists had been extremely active (3, 6, 7). Socialist participation and the attitudes of the 'new' unions' leaders indicated to Cole that the 'New Unions were in intention Socialist' committed to a 'fighting policy based upon class solidarity and directed, by implication at any rate, against the capitalist system itself' (51).

Different in ideology, different in tactics, different in organisation? Often the 'new union' had the word 'general' in its title and in this sense could be seen as reviving the idea of the One Big Union of all the working classes, breaking away finally from the sectionalism of the old unions. A 'general' union would take as its recruitment area the whole of the British labouring force. Labourers who went on strike could easily be replaced by other labourers, so the new general unions must bring all labourers within their control to prevent the use of blacklegs in disputes. Theoretically the recruits would belong to the floating mass of interchangeable workers whose interests could be protected and promoted by the union. As such men were unlikely to have in themselves much industrial weight the organisers of the 'new unions' looked to political action and gave support to such demands as Tom Mann's proposal of a legal eight-hour day, put forward in his pamphlet in 1886. This model had some validity for the 'new unions' formed in the first trade union explosion of 1889-92, but in the face of recession and employer counterattack in the 1890s the 'new unions' best survived with pockets of semi-skilled in regular employment who were relatively difficult to replace. Even what Tom Mann had called 'the true unionist policy of aggression' increasingly gave way to trade policies not markedly distinct from the policies of the older unions.

Within British industry the union man with his power to bargain with his employer or membership of a conciliation board, with his guaranteed friendly society benefits represented a privileged minority and by the mid-1880s other working groups were seeking to secure similar privileges. The first was the National Labour Federation on Tyneside in 1886, then the National Seamen's and Firemen's Union in 1887 and the Liverpool dockers' union in 1889. The first great success was amongst the gas workers, where Will Thorne, a Birmingham born gas worker and a socialist, secured an eight-hour day at the Beckton Gas Works in East Ham in 1889, a victory for his newly created National Union of Gasworkers.

In all these 'new unions' certain special causes may be seen to be operating: in the docks greater competition between the dock companies and the speeding up of the whole process of loading and unloading which began with the steam ship; in the gas industry. Hobsbawn (116) has analysed the impact on the worker of the 'iron man', a mechanical means of fuelling and drawing off the residual coke. One general cause was the overall improvement in trade which made effective union action possible.

The London dock strike of 1889 looked like a test case for the 'new unionism'. As a potential source of unionisation, dockers looked extremely unlikely, and the Dickensian conditions of the 'call-ons' [doc. 13] made them the supreme example of the replaceable mobile labourer. Within the industry, a labour aristocracy existed in the stevedores, who had the monopoly of loading, a more highly skilled job than unloading, and at many docks there were also middlemen employing gangs. At the bottom men were working on average four hours a day at five pence an hour, low even by East End standards. How could these ill-paid part-timers be organised into a fighting union? And if a union were established, how could it be maintained?

The immediate cause of the strike mattered little; the list of grievances was formidable. The gasworkers' success was a direct inspiration to men who were often dockers in the summer and gas workers in the winter. The dockers were fortunate in having Ben Tillett as their leader, a superb organiser and tactician. Tillett submitted demands which he called 'a first step towards decasualisation of dock labour', a first step based upon a wage increase from fivepence to sixpence an hour with eightpence for overtime [doc. 14].

Tillett started with powerful allies: the better paid dockworkers, the stevedores, London's most famous socialists – H.H. Champion, John Burns, Tom Mann, Eleanor Marx-Aveling – Karl Marx's daughter, Annie Besant and the London press, notably *The Star* and *The Times*. One other great advantage was the goodwill of the London public, partly won over by the impressive and peaceful processions which wound each day from the docks to Tower Hill, carefully marshalled by Ben Tillett and his strike committee.

The struggle lasted in all for five weeks and the dockers were helped to survive by financial aid from other trade unions and wellwishers. £49,000 was subscribed to give them victory, of which £30,000 came from Australian trade unionists. Without this assistance the strikers might have been forced to try to rally other unions for a general strike, a move which might risk the goodwill they had won.

Financial help and the emergence of the Mansion House Committee, prominently led by the Lord Mayor Sydney Buxton and Cardinal Manning, were the two major factors which brought success. Manning was not only a skilled tactician but also a man whose gentleness and compassion won the hearts of the dockers. It was Manning who worked out a compromise conceding most of the dockers' demands and then persuaded both sides to accept it. The dockers got their pay increases, 'the dockers' tanner'. From the struggle emerged the Dockers' Union, with a membership of 30,000, with Ben Tillett as secretary and Tom Man as President. More than anything else the London dock strike had demonstrated what could be achieved by disciplined, resolute men with a good case, public sympathy and sufficient funds.

The Dockers' Union rose to 40,000 in 1890 and then dropped away to a mere 10,000 in 1910. The union's highly centralised constitution showed the handiwork of Tom Mann, a tribute perhaps to his own ignorance of the powerful traditions of local autonomy which dominated the waterfront workers. The 1890s was a particularly hazardous decade for the union, faced by the new Shipping Federation committed to extirpating unionism in the docks and at sea and aided by a trade depression which made mere survival difficult. To maintain a union at all in these circumstances was no mean task and the human material was peculiarly intractable. Dockers were notoriously hostile to organisation and had a tradition of aggressive independence. In the 1889 strike key support had come from the stevedores, whose union achieved full employer recognition; after 1889 the stevedores maintained their own independence from the new union and indeed rejected an offer of amalgamation with the Dockers' Union, from which they had little or nothing to gain **(21)**.

The geographical strength of the Dockers' Union shifted from London to Bristol where there was a nucleus of stable members, with a strong section in the South Wales tinplate workers. Most branches were in the south-west, whence grew the National Transport Workers' Federation in 1910, the forerunner of the Transport and General Workers' Union **(8)**.

Will Thorne's Gasworkers proved to be another survivor. In 1890, the great year, Thorne had over 60,000 on his books; by 1892 the union had rather less than 23,000. Thorne's own militancy was blunted by the decline in trade and he was advising his members to be 'very judicious ... in treating with employers in matters connected with work and wages' **(36)**. Towards the end of the decade the union began once more to expand, due mainly to a determined policy of bringing in builders' labourers. The geographical coverage of the union was also shifting away from London to large towns such as Birmingham.

One general union, the Workers' Union, arose from the humiliating defeat of the engineers in the Terms of Settlement (1899). The moving spirit was Tom Mann who argued the case for its creation in the *Weekly Times and Echo*. It must, he said, 'be a political union', and able 'to show an utter disregard of Liberal and Tory, and go purely for Labour'.

The new union was to pick up members from those 'hundreds of thousands of men who have to change their occupation a dozen times or more in as many years' (47).

The new union had no easy birth. Its political vision was treated with suspicion by existing socialist parties, the Social Democratic Federation and the Independent Labour Party and its industrial purpose bitterly criticised by fellow trade unionists. In their view there were enough unions. What was lacking was working class participation. Mann's initial expectations that the Workers' union would enrol 15,000 proved wildly unrealistic: within the first year there were just over 4,000 members. A flexibility of policy which was to a major characteristic led the union to adjust its sights. The dream of enrolling the mobile working man was slowly abandoned as the union offered both funeral benefits and optional friendly society benefits, and the union survived with the support of men in regular employment. Membership stood at around 5,000 until the great expansion of 1911-14, but ironically, despite its late entry into the field the Workers' Union by the turn of the century was the fourth largest of the general unions.

Did the socialism of the early leaders affect the long-term strategy of the 'new unions'? G.D.H. Cole argues that 'their leaders denounced friendly benefits as leading to stagnation' yet new unions, even the Workers' Union did offer friendly society benefits and as Clegg, Fox and Thompson argue (36) 'there is no set pattern', the 'new' unions policies depended on 'the realistic calculation of tactical possibilities and bargaining strengths'. The survival of general unions in the 1890s depended on two unrelated conditions: employer recognition, which gave a cogent reason for belonging, and industrial diversification. It was essential to have hard cores of regularly employed members in different industries so that defeat or decline in one industry could be offset by branches elsewhere.

In organisation, socialism, as John Lovell points out (59), failed to break down the sectionalism of the unions – the basic problems of the shop floor, concerned with conditions of employment, wage rates and demarcation, diminished the relevance of an ideology which trade unionists saw as having little to say on the bread-and-butter problems of their own lives. Many of the new unions became increasingly exclusive, for the ideal proletarian, able and willing to take on any unskilled job was not easy to discover. The new unions 'depended far more on their foothold in certain industries and large works than on their ability to recruit indiscriminately'.

The new unions came more and more to look like the old unions in their policies, particularly when they came up against the problems of control of more militant branches, the problem which had forced the amalgamated societies to supervise so closely the trade policies of the union as a whole. If local branches fell into dispute with employers, the union faced the possibility of crippling financial loss, and in the event of a defeat, the rapid decline of the branch.

'New unionism' did, however, produce change. According to the Webbs, sixty new trade councils were established between 1889-91, a remarkable expansion of 'municipal' industrial activity. Within the TUC itself where the new men first appeared in 1890, John Burns has told us that 'they looked like workmen; they were workmen', and these were the men who pushed the TUC towards supporting the movement for the legal eight-hour day, a movement which seemed to symbolise many things for which 'new unionism' stood, in particular the use of the power of the state to secure economic improvement.

'New unionism' also offered support to women workers in industry, although women's trade unionism went back to the work of Mrs Emma Paterson who in 1874 set up the Women's Protective and Provident League and who was elected to the TUC in 1875. Her league helped to foster several women's trade societies and in 1882 there was a separate women's organisation in London, the London Women's Trade Council. The most signal success of the women's movement was the London match girls' strike in 1888 and the new unions set up after 1888 normally made membership open to women. The most successful was the Workers' Union which employed effective and militant women organisers. The new atmosphere is best evidenced by the acceptance of the doctrine of equal pay for equal work in 1885 by the TUC but apart from such areas as the textile industry where in weaving women membership had always been strongly encouraged, women in industry were still largely unorganised up to the Great War (45).

Even traditional craft unions such as the ASE found the going rough within an industry affected not only by change in world trade but change also in engineering technology. The introduction of new machines, such as the capstan and the turret lathe had encouraged employers to engage non-union labour at lower rates, for the new equipment did not need the traditional skilled engineer. The union executive were prepared to find ways to bring in the machineminders but the shop floor workers bitterly defended their privileges and their relative bargaining position against intruders, supported as Clegg, Fox and Thompson point out by socialists committed to ending all privilege. One other threat to their status was the growing use of piecework payment. In some branches of engineering this new method of payment grew very rapidly indeed. In 1886, for instance, only 6 per cent of turners and fitters were paid in this way, but by 1906 the proportion had risen to 33 per cent.

Within the ASE itself there was a divide appearing between those who saw the union as a safeguard against the normal disasters of a working man's life and those who had been won over by the new militancy. In 1891 the election of a general secretary brought Tom Mann himself into the field, and in a hard-fought election he was narrowly defeated. The meeting of delegates at Leeds in 1892 brought victory of another kind to the militants, for the historic constitution of the ASE was transformed, replacing the old London-based union by a national union, with eight electoral districts electing full time officials who were to comprise the executive. To widen the basis of the union and specifically to bring in the new machinists, the ASE devised a new category of membership, a purpose hardly fulfilled by the 4,500 special members who were ASE members in 1898 from a total membership of 91,000. However small the harvest, the ASE had been forced to move towards the concept of an identity of interests between the skilled and the semi-skilled, a step towards a general union in the engineering industry.

In the 1890s Britain's economic hegemony was increasingly challenged by the rise of German and American competition; depression reappeared sharply in 1892; the great expansion of 1890-91 when trade union membership doubled was halted. In some industries such as cotton, men like David Holmes, the amalgamated weavers' President, were accepting the fact of competition as the new context in which their industrial strategy should be developed, a sense of industrial partnership promising for the future of the industry.

From 750,000 in 1888 trade union membership grew to 1.5 million in 1892, declined during the period 1893-96 and then began to rise again to reach over a million by 1901. In some industries trade union membership showed spectacular growth. In mining, for instance, in 1888 trade union density stood at 19 per cent and at 56 per cent in 1901; in shipbuilding, too, it rose from 36 per cent to 60 per cent. Elsewhere, although there was some growth, the overall percentage trade union membership was small: in engineering a rise from 15 to 21 per cent and in railways from 9 to 24 per cent. By 1900 new unionism had only just begun to make its mark and new unionists only accounted for 10 per cent of all trade unionists. At the beginning of the twentieth century the strongholds of trade unionism were still the same as in 1888: engineering, building, shipbuilding, printing, mining and cotton. King Coal, King Cotton and the craft unions still dominated the trade union world. The 'new unions' with their militancy and their socialist leaders, had failed to achieve that continuing expansion which in the immediate aftermath of the dock strike had seemed so likely.

7 The Counter-attack

By the 1890s there are clear signs of an employers' counterattack on the growing strength of the unions. Clegg, Fox and Thompson (36) draw attention to the fact 'that the most significant event of 1890, as of 1889, occurred in the London docks. . . . Tillett's union was eased out of the docks with scarcely a ripple of public interest.' This reversal of fortune happened after a series of unsuccessful stoppages. By the end of that year the newly-won union power of negotiating piece rates was already lost, and employers had gone back to their old system, thus depriving the unions of their foothold in fixing wages and conditions. Counterattack there was too in the growth of employers' federations, in the use of 'free labour', in the new hard line which produced the spinners' strike of 1892, the miners' strike of 1893 and the engineering lockout of 1897. J. Saville (91) has argued that the industrial events of the 1890s must be seen in the context of 'a developing counterattack by the propertied classes against the industrial organisations of the working people'. The employers' hostility was evidenced by *The Times* in its frequent comments on trade unions. Many shared the viewpoint of the National Federation of Associated Employers of Labour, which included such industrial magnates as Harland, the shipbuilder (of Harland and Wolf), Titus Salt of Bradford, and Thomas Vickers. This Federation, formed in 1873, saw unions as 'making rules for other men's businesses' and 'dominating workshops', and complained that they 'do all but take possession of plant and capital'. Unions ran counter to mid-Victorian liberalism and were fundamentally in restraint of trade; furthermore they were taking away from workmen the essential freedom of selling his own labour to his own employer. The 1890s saw the persistence of such attitudes – indeed they have not even now entirely disappeared – but the important development was the growing willingness of employers, particularly in those industries where unions were long established, to deal with trade unions through a process of collective bargaining or through established conciliation machinery. Employers were less anxious, both in those industries and in others, to deal with newly established unions representing working groups of inferior respectability to the old societies of craftsmen or the unions of selected groups in spinning, or in the iron trades.

Trade union growth encouraged employers to look for an organisation with which to fight unions, to preserve prerogatives such as control of the composition of the labour force which employers held were rightly theirs. For established trade unions these new employer federations had advantages, as negotiated agreements would have nationwide acceptance and there would be no need to fight different battles at different times and places to secure the same end. Their disadvantages to the unions were equally clear: with their combined economic strength they could impose policies on weaker unions, or withstand strikes even by more powerful and financially secure unions, with no fundamental damage to their own members. The Shipping Federation, newly created in 1890, was very quickly able to crush the seamen's union.

One other development, less promising for industrial peace was the market in 'free labour' for strike breaking. In the older unions, imported labour could not be used to break a strike for there was no alternative skilled labour available. At the end of a strike, whoever won, craftsmen went back to their original jobs, and this was accepted by both sides to the dispute. No similar assumption could be made by unions recruiting from semi-skilled or unskilled labour. A strike could readily put many jobs at risk. Employers, particularly in the docks, would rapidly bring in blacklegs. In the early 1890s various associations already existed to meet the employers' needs for free labour and in 1893 an ex-trade unionist, William Collison, with backing from the Shipping Federation, built up a national service, the National Free Labour Association, to move men to wherever they were needed to replace strikers.

Collison based the NFLA on 'the right possessed by every man to pursue his Trade or Employment without dictation, molestation or obstruction', and central to his scheme was the Free Labour pledge by which workmen agreed to work with union and non-union workers without distinction. Throughout the country Collison set up in each district a Free Labour Exchange to keep an up-to-date list of men willing to be employed in what was normally strike breaking.

The NFLA carried on propaganda against union activities in general and picketing in particular: it offered a service to employers and with the financial backing of employers provided within the industrial field a demonstration of the virtues of a free market in labour at a time when employers and *The Times* were becoming increasingly convinced that the growth of trade unionism was a threat to the well-being of the economy. The arguments for 'taking on the unions' steeped in traditional economic theory seemed stronger and were more widely accepted than the case for conciliation (**91**).

On the employers side the new organisational strength of the ASE was met by the setting up in 1894 of the Federation of Employers'

Associations and within three years a major confrontation took place. Ostensibly the dispute arose over a move to call for an eight-hour day but behind this lay the anxieties and stresses caused by the changes taking place in the industry. A new general secretary, George Barnes, supported by Tom Mann and his sympathisers in the union, joined forces in London with the Boilermakers, the Patternmakers and thirteen other smaller unions to campaign for an eight-hour day. In May 1897 the Joint Committee submitted their proposals to the London employers with some immediate success. In this critical situation, the Employers' Federation, which previously had had little support in London, won over the London employers and persuaded them to resist. The Joint Committee unions called their men out in early July and the Employers' Federation then showed their strength by shifting the fight to the country at large by ordering their members to lock out all trade union members of the London Joint Committee throughout the country. Such a national lockout was unprecedented. Its effect was catastrophic: 17,000 trade unionists were affected immediately; by October nearly 45,000 men were locked out, of whom 22,000 were ASE members. The strike lasted for six months, with little public interest. Support came not from the TUC Parliamentary Committee, which seemed unconcerned, but from other trade unions, and in particular from the German trade union movement (through the help of Eleanor Marx-Aveling) which subscribed nearly half of the £28,000 given by fraternal unions.

The two factions offered different interpretations of the ASE's defeat. The friendly society men saw the defeat as a product of the new militancy and the strike itself as a gross squandering of union funds. The militants argued that the concession of defeat was made too soon with the union's funds still standing at £134,000.

The terms of the settlement gave the employers the whip-hand. The union had to abandon a closed shop policy, their claim to control the number of apprentices and their opposition to piecework. The ASE's sense of desertion by the TUC in its hour of need led to the engineers withdrawing from the TUC until 1905. As an alternative the ASE joined the General Federation of Trade Unions set up in 1899, in the hope, not in fact fulfilled, that this association would be more vigorous than the Parliamentary Committee.

The ASE did not really recover from the great lockout in the years before the Great War. Nor, on the other hand, did the union take sufficient advantage of the great expansion of the engineering industry in those years. From slightly more than a million workers at the turn of the century the industry grew to an employment roll of 1¾ million by 1911. The ASE had grown from 70,000 in 1892 to 170,000 in 1914, a far from dramatic improvement. The hold of the traditional craft worker in the union turning on a narrow definition of engineer is reflected in the analysis that J.B Jeffreys gives of membership. In 1865 79 per cent of the ASE members were either fitters or turners; in 1914, although ninety-three trades could be recruited, 90 per cent of the members were fitters or turners. In its search to protect its members the ASE had achieved only a narrow basis in a rapidly expanding industry.

Cotton factory owners, like engineering employers, created a federation in order to deal more effectively with the union. Faced by a series of intractable stoppages, employers in Ashton, Oldham and Manchester set up in 1891 the Federation of Master Spinners' Association. It covered initially almost half the total spinning capacity of the industry.

The Federation was first used in 1892 when the employers proposed a 5 per cent reduction in pay. When James Mawdsley, the spinners' union secretary, rejected the proposal, the Federation closed all their mills. The spinners, with a wealthy union and good leadership, settled down for a long struggle. In all the dispute lasted from November 1892 to March 1893 and was ended by commonsense on both sides. In the Brooklands Agreement – named after the hotel where the agreement was signed – the spinners agreed to accept a reduction of slightly under 3 per cent and both management and men accepted a general agreement controlling wages, with provision for proper procedures for collective bargaining and negotiation. The new procedures were often laborious and slow-moving but they did provide a period of industrial peace.

In weaving, the acceptance of the Uniform List in 1892 by unions and management prevented any major stoppage over wages. Indeed in the years between 1894 and 1900 'there was no dispute of any size' (36).

For mining the 1890s were years of expansion and growth for trade unionism with the Miners' Federation moving into new areas and emerging by the turn of the century as a union able to speak on behalf of most of the miners in England, Scotland and Wales. The MFGB proved more successful than the miners of the north-east in protecting their members' interests. Their initial campaign concentrated on proposals for restrictions on output and support for the TUC's demand for an eight-hour day. However, as output increased and prices fell, mine owners called for a cut in wages. To meet this pressure, the union leaders insisted that no Federation members should accept reductions in wages without consent from the Federation, on pain of immediate expulsion. During the decade this tough policy led to great hardship amongst some groups of miners who suffered lockout from mineowners as a consequence.

One such lockout in Durham, where the union still accepted the sliding scale and were outside the Federation, lasted for twelve weeks in 1892. The MFGB subscribed £42,000 to the Durham miners' strike fund, almost half the total. In gratitude for their support the Durham pitmen joined the Federation, only to withdraw again in 1893 over policy. Northumberland, which had followed Durham in, also followed Durham out.

By 1893 only the MFGB had successfully protected wages against forced reductions but in midsummer the union was faced by a mineowners demand for a 25 per cent reduction in wages against the background of a price fall of 35 per cent. A special conference of miners voted against acceptance. In the last week of July the mineowners locked out the colliers and immediately 300,000 miners were without work. The lockout was marked by the arrival in mining districts of 'newly imported soldiers and police' (31). There was one particularly ugly incident at Featherstone, near Wakefield, where a local magistrate and colliery owner called for soldiers from York. During the day the soldiers fired on an unarmed crowd, killing two and wounding sixteen others. A coroner's jury found 'that James Gibb was killed by a bullet wound, inflicted by soldiers ... and that, since James Gibb was a peaceful man took no part in any riotous proceedings, the jury record their sympathy with the deceased relatives and friends'.

This miners' lockout made history in that it led to direct intervention by government. It lasted fifteen weeks with increasing effects on industry until finally Gladstone wrote to the MFGB's general secretary [doc. 15]. The government sponsored a joint meeting, with the Foreign Secretary Lord Rosebery in the chair, and the men were allowed to return to work at their original wage, a major victory for the Federation. From this meeting stemmed a Concilliation Board originally empowered to settle wages for a year, and then extended for a further three years. For the MFGB 1893 marked success for their stand, with an effective defence of their wages at a time when non-Federation miners faced continuing reductions.

In 1894 the Federation was linked with the Scottish Miners' Federation, leaving only the north-east and South Wales as areas where their writ did not run. Eventually, after a disastrous stoppage in 1898, the frontiers between England and Wales crumbled. Paradoxically, after an owners' victory, union strength in South Wales increased with the formation of the South Wales Miners' Federation. In 1899 William

Abraham, normally known by his Bardic name of Mabon (1), the Welsh miners' leader, describing himself and his supporters as 'penitent Welshmen' sought to join up with the MFBG. The Welsh miners came in and the Welsh Miners' Federation by the turn of the century had 128,000 members, roughly a third of the MFGB's total membership.

8 Trade Unions and Politics

THE GROWTH OF POLITICAL AWARENESS

Apart from rare men such as George Potter, Victorian trade unionists did not see trade unions as having a wide political role. The function of a trade union was to improve the condition of life of its members. Differences arose as to tactics and in particular the different emphasis placed on militant action. Differences there were over membership and qualifications for membership, but political action was almost universally seen as concerned with the creation of parliamentary pressure groups to bring in legislation to improve conditions of work. If trade unionists had a political allegiance it would be to the Liberal Party, to the Party of Progress rather than the Conservative Party, the Party of Order. When after the Reform Acts of 1867 and 1884 the working-class vote grew enormously in importance, the Liberal Party evolved the policy of putting up working-class men as Liberal candidates in predominantly working-class constituencies, a policy which was not very successful.

Trade unionists had two different political traditions to draw on: Owenism and Chartism. Owenism had provided a programme of co-operation based on the concept of a society in which members would work together for the common good and industry and social life would be based on mutual cooperation. The strength of this tradition was to be shown in its emergence in William Morris's powerful writings in *News from Nowhere,* which modified the Owenite vision by Morris's own call for a return to a tradition of craftsmanship and peasant community. Chartism with its emphasis on class consciousness and its vigorous call for a true political democracy had largely become irrelevant with the late Victorian Reform Bills. In neither of these two major political reforms had trade unions as such played an important part. Indeed working-class participation was more obviously displayed in trade unions and in industrial activity than in politics.

In the 1880s new ideas began to emerge about social ownership of the means of production stemming initially from the middle classes, from Morris himself, from Hyndman and H.H. Champion, and beyond that from the Fabians – Shaw, Wells and the Webbs. It might be possible to see the late nineteenth century 'Great Depression' as a direct cause of socialist activity but this could lead to an undue emphasis on the extent and effect of that recession on trade union attitudes, even upon workers in general. Even in the years of depression, real wages increased steadily: A.L. Bowley estimates that the average real wage rose by 35 per cent between 1880 and 1890 and by another 7 per cent by 1896 (55). As late as 1895, the TUC were devising procedural obstacles to prevent socialism within the trade union movement from affecting the electoral fortunes of the Liberals.

To a society as class-ridden and hierarchical as nineteenth century England, ideas of transfer of social control were extremely remote. English trade unionists shared the general view of the constant base of English society: it is striking how remote they were in this way from their continental brothers. In Germany, in France, and in Spain, trade unions had a base in revolutionary politics, and were normally Marxist or Bakuninist. Discussion turned on the nature of the new society which would emerge in the post-revolutionary period. The English distinction between a trade union with industrial objectives and a working-class party with political objectives was not accepted in continental working men's associations. What was fundamental was the achievement of working-class solidarity by watever means were to hand. Over European working-class movements stood the dominant figure of Karl Marx but although Marx lived in London until his death in 1883, paradoxically he had little influence on English trade unionism (62).

To Marx the essential move was the creation of an independent working men's party to achieve political power for the working class, a view that he had proclaimed in the inaugural address to the International Working Men's Association in 1864 in London. The political potential of such a party had been evidenced by 1877 when the Marxist Social Democratic Party in Germany won thirteen seats in the Reichstag and went on to gain thirty-five seats in 1890.

Within England, too, there was in the 1880s an intellectual atmosphere favouring the rise of a collectivist party. The *laissez faire* state had been proved wanting in a whole range of matters, from child prostitution to housing, and in 1875 the Conservative government had strengthened the state power in sanitation, and in housing and hospitals. Competitive capitalism no longer guaranteed a permanently rising standard of life for the middle classes, as the rise of German and American industry brought about a decline in profits. The state might now be needed not merely to maintain public order but also to protect living standards.

English socialism in the 1880s was not only distinctly middle-class but socialists were thin on the ground. There were perhaps at most two thousand listed members of the various socialist groups, the Fabians, the Social Democratic Federation, the Socialist League. Members, however, were usually articulate and had time and money to spend on the cause. In terms of relationship with the trade unions the most important group was the SDF, a party which was largely the brainchild of H.M. Hyndman, a wealthy Cambridge graduate whose family fortune had been made in the West Indies. Hyndman was converted to Marxism in the 1880s by a reading of Marx's *Capital*. When first founded, the SDF was a radical organisation concerned mainly with 'the question of improvement in the social condition of the people'. Under Hyndman's guidance it proclaimed a programme of nationalisation which was to include 'all the means of production, distribution and exchange' (56).

The SDF recruited Tom Mann and John Burns, both of whom had taken an active part in the major strikes of 1888 and 1889. Will Thorne and Ben Tillett both became members. Under the difficult leadership of Hyndman the SDF had a fluctuating membership, with factions breaking away, such as the group led by William Morris which formed the Socialist League. However the dedicated support given by individual socialists in the strikes which created the 'new unions' had great propaganda value for the socialists.

But the socialist impulse which was to carry English trade unionists to the point of accepting the need for independent labour representation in the Commons came, not from the SDF nor from the socialist representatives who entered the Congress in 1890 on the waves of new unionism, but from the Independent Labour Party and its extraordinary founder, Keir Hardie.

James Keir Hardie had begun work as a miner at the age of eight in his native Lanarkshire and had become increasingly involved in trade union activity. He was sacked for his trade union activities and he set about creating the Ayrshire Miners' Federation while working as a journalist. A Liberal by conviction, initially he became attracted by Henry George and also by the SDF. On a miners delegation to London in 1887 he made contact with the SDF, and met Eleanor Marx and Engels. He became a socialist but did not join the SDF and in 1888 he became the miners' parliamentary candidate for Mid-Lanark. Hardie asked for the Liberal vote but the local Liberal Association refused it and put up their own candidate. The Mid-Lanark by-election became a national concern and Hardie brought London socialists, including H.H. Champion, to speak on his behalf, but in the end he only polled 617 votes. Hardie had not fought on a socialist platform but one not dissimilar from other Radical candidates: the election was of historic importance because local liberals had blocked the adoption of a local candidate in favour of a London barrister rather than for its end result. Hardie had had the support of the Labour Electoral Association founded by the TUC itself to get working men into parliament and his failure to get the Liberal nomination decided him to break with the LEA and in 1888 to create a new body, the Scottish Labour Party, with a broadly based programme of labour reforms, rather than of socialism. He ran as an independent candidate in West Ham South with local Radical backing but without accepting the formal Liberal ticket, and in the general election of 1892 he won the seat with a majority of over a thousand. (the only other independent candidate returned was John Burns for Battersea.) Hardie had made a very important political point: that working men could win parliamentary seats without standing as an official candidate for one of the two main parties.

In the autumn of 1892 at the Glasgow TUC Keir Hardie organised the calling of a conference at Bradford from which sprang a national ILP constructed along trade union lines, with a national conference to control the party. Hardie's diplomatic chairmanship guided the meeting towards the acceptance of a constitution congenial and familiar to trade unionists, and which reflected the general view of the delegates that an Independent Labour Party must be based solidly on the unique institution of the working class, the trade unions.

Within the trade union movement the strongest support for the Lib-Lab idea came from the miners who were to prove difficult to shift from their entrenched positions. The miners' opposition was expressed in the TUC, in its Parliamentary Committee, and by miner MPs. The miners' unions' parliamentary record was extremely impressive: the first working men in the Commons, Alexander Macdonald (elected at Stafford) and Thomas Burt (Morpeth) were both miners returned after the General Election of 1874. In every election five or six miners would be returned and even at the height of Lib-Labism, normally half the Lib-Lab MPs returned would be miners.

At the miners' conference in 1884 the miners' unions outlined their position. 'It is impossible', they said, 'for anybody but a working man to put before the House of Commons working men's views, feelings and conditions'. Furthermore they said a national fund was 'visionary and impracticable'. 'Working men' in their view, 'must be sent to Parliament by trades organisations . . . selected by a trade . . . and [as] a paid official of such trades organisation.' Working men in Parliament must then work with the Liberal Party to secure reforms in their own interest. The strength of miners' opposition to Keir Hardie's ILP led miners' MPs such as Charles Fenwick to campaign against the ILP in defence of one Lib-Lab alliance. If labour legislation was to get through the House, it must be through the agency of the Liberal Party and not through the activities of visionaries and dreamers.

The other bastion of Lib-Lab ideas was the TUC Parliamentary Committee set up as a watchdog in 1871 over the Trade Union Bill but now gradually evolving into a General Council of the trade union movement. The TUC's subsequent strategy had been to use the Parliamentary Committee as its instrument for improving legislation and from 1875, as the Committee's secretary, Henry Broadhurst, ex-stonemason and now a Liberal MP helped to give its dominant characteristic in this period, a cautious conservatism. Its programme was based on limited reform, not too dissimilar from that of the radical wing of the Liberal Party, and including such proposals as the appointment of 'practical' men as factory inspectors and the abolition of imprisonment for debt. The programme's main plank was a demand for an Employers' Liability Bill, which in a limited form found its way to the statute book in 1880.

After the extension of the suffrage in 1884 the Parliamentary Committee submitted to the TUC an election manifesto based on eleven points, all modest and practical, starting with a proposal for an improvement of the 1880 Employers' Liability Act. Whatever else the Parliamentary Committee might be accused of, it could not be accused of rocking the national boat. Certainly it was no easy task to frame a programme which might win general TUC approval, for the textile unions were solidly conservative and the programme had to be one which would offend neither Liberal nor Conservative.

From 1886 onwards the Committee found itself under increasing pressure from advocates of the new socialist ideas influencing small groups of workmen and trade unionists in the country. At his first appearance at the TUC, in 1887, Keir Hardie challenged the Committee, and the TUC's President, a Welsh socialist named Bevan, roundly asserted that 'we recognise our most serious evils in the unrestrained, unscrupulous and remorseless forces of capitalism'.

With the resignation of Henry Broadhurst in 1890 an era in the Committee's history ended. Both he and the Parliamentary Committee itself had been representative of a trade union movement based on the skilled worker, a movement which represented no more than a half a million workers in the country. The rise of the 'new unionism' and the success of the dock strike were to bring a new type of trade unionist to Congress, more militant, often socialist, and bitterly critical of the complacency of the older unions. However there was no easy and inevitable movement from the formation of the ILP in 1893 to the creation of the Labour Representation Committee in 1900: winning over the TUC to the principle of an independent labour party was a difficult task, made more complex by personal rivalries and by changes in TUC procedure. This was made more urgent by the increasing evidence of the isolation of trade unions under the Salisbury Conservative administration and the new efforts of employers to use the existing legal machinery and new institutions like the National Free Labour Association to confront the growing strength of the unions.

The change in TUC procedure which led to the exclusion of Keir Hardie was made on the initiative of John Burns, increasingly resentful of the growing influence of the new independent MP. Within the TUC Hardie, with his vision of a splendid socialist future and his patent integrity, was becoming a powerful figure. Burns proposed a small TUC committee to revise Standing Orders and Burns himself became a member. The committee's report recommended a series of important changes, in particular that trades councils, increasingly under socialist influence, should not send delegates to Conference, and that anyone who was not working at his trade or was not a paid trade union organiser should be excluded. This last clause would have the effect of excluding Broadhurst, Burns, Burt, Hardie and Mann. Burns was prepared to sacrifice his own position to remove Keir Hardie. The Parliamentary Committee (where the proposals were only carried by the chairman's casting vote) was concerned to protect the Liberal interest against the new challenge from the socialists.

One other change had taken place in procedure which strengthened the antisocialist camp: the introduction of a system of card voting by which the number of votes assigned to a union in congress would be a direct reflection of the size of the union's membership. This procedural change replaced the old system by which trade unions could send the number of representatives they thought appropriate and put power in the hands of the coal and textile unions, which were unsympathetic to the concept of independent labour representation in the Commons (34).

For many trade unionists to create a political, independent role for the trade union movement would bring British trade unions disastrously near their continental counterparts and would help to split unions with committed conservative members. Why within five years had the mood of Congress so altered? Its early opposition is understandable in view of the sectional interests which unions pursued, circumvented to a greater or lesser degree at the time of a strike which often called on the support of unions in other trades. Within a free capitalist society, trade unions by free collective bargaining, and where need be by other pressures such as strike action, made the best possible bargain for their members. If a basically liberal society became a basically socialist society this might produce a worsening of conditions for some trade union groups in order to improve the lot of others. Trade unionists had shown themselves committed to the differential – there was no wish to see that eroded. Egalitarianism, either economic or social, was not a very strong force in working-class life. Indeed at Congress there had been scenes of open hostility between members from the new unions and representatives of the older unions of skilled workers. What was finally to swing TUC opinion to the side of independent representation in Parliament by a narrow majority (546,000 to 434,000) was the weakness of their position in the face of courts and employers.

For employers, for British industry generally, the 1890s were a period of falling profits. German and American industry were expanding faster than British industry and technological inventiveness, once the outstanding characteristic of British industry, seemed to have diminished, if not departed. Joseph Chamberlain was already advocating the idea of an imperial tariff (77) and since 1881 the National Fair Trade League had been pressing for the abandonment of free trade in the interests of Britain's own manufacturers. Protection against unfair competition from abroad; protection from unfair practices at home through employers' federations, the revival of the technique of lockout, and the use of blackleg labour with the organised help of William Collison – these were increasingly the characteristics of British industry in the 1890s.

In the courts decisions were handed down reducing the power of trade unions in strikes, of which Lyons *v* Wilkins (1896) was the most significant. In this decision the right to picket to dissuade men from working for a strike bound employer was denied and the 1875 law on picketing was thereby circumscribed. The case had another quite different importance: it was not taken to appeal to the Lords because the Parliamentary Committee of the TUC had no ready source of funds to fight even such a case as this with its clearly threatening implications for the whole of the trade union movement. This weakness added strength to the demand that some more powerful lobby than the Parliamentary Committee was needed to defend the movement's interests.

With Chamberlain's own genuine interest in social reform now abandoned in favour of colonial problems and South Africa, the Salisbury government showed no further interest in such matters as old age pensions. When the TUC met in 1899 a general election was pending and ILP member of the Amalgamated Society of Railway Servants moved a resolution to call a congress to find ways of increasing the number of labour members in Parliament [doc. 16]. Despite the opposition of the Miners' Federation and the Cotton Spinners, the resolution was carried. On February 17, 1900 a conference of 129 delegates met in London, at the Memorial Hall in Farringdon Street. The conference represented only roughly one-third of the trade union movement, with support coming mainly from railwaymen, the engineers, the gasworkers and the boot and shoe operatives. It was this conference which decided to set up the Labour Representation Committee of seven trade union representatives, with two others from the ILP, two from the Social Democratic Federation and one Fabian. Keir Hardie's dream of a party drawing its strength from the organised working class was on the way to realisation, and the fairly speedy withdrawal of the SDF helped to affirm the ideal of a trade union party with some socialist members (54).

TAFF VALE AND THE LRC

The Taff Vale railway brought coal from the Welsh mining valleys down to the ports of Cardiff and Barry. The South African war had stimulated the prosperity of a normally prosperous line; profits were rising but not wages. Wartime inflation had increased prices but the Taff Vale railway workers had had no wage increases to offset the rising cost of living. A general discontent on the wage question in a strongly unionised railway was the groundswell which helped to produce the strike which began in August 1900. There were other local factors, too. Against his own wishes, John Ewington, an active union organiser was moved to a new district. Another factor was the presence of James Holmes, the area ASRS organiser, who had in 1899 moved a resolution at the TUC calling for independent political representation in the Commons. It should also be borne in mind that as elsewhere on the railways management did not recognise the unions. Apart from Ewington's case the strike had two main aims: union recognition and an increased wage. At headquarters Richard Bell, the general secretary, was counselling caution to Holmes, but the Taff Vale signalmen did not know that Holmes and Bell were not at one over the strike. Initially 350 railmen handed in their notices but this original nucleus built up to around 800 when signalmen, guards and brakemen were joined by drivers and firemen, who acted without giving prior warning to the company. By a vote of seven to five, the strike just managed to get official backing.

Normally the stoppage of so many skilled men would have been crippling to the rail company but an appeal to Collison's National Free Labour Association proved lucky, for they had a reserve of skilled men and with the help of free labour the passenger trains were running normally again. But not the coal trains: the rail strike had a catastrophic effect on the miners and very quickly thousands were standing idle. Nevertheless they were behind the strike, backed up by the local paper, the *South Wales Daily News*. With the help of Bell's skill and a local industrialist, Sir William Thomas Lewis, a settlement was reached. But the strike failed in its objectives and even Ewington had his case referred to a Board of Trade tribunal.

If the matter had ended there, Taff Vale might have gone down as a hastily conceived strike, with much justice on the strikers' side, but which had ended badly, with blackleg labour still working the trains. The losses to the company were around £20,000 and to South Wales as a whole as much as £400,000. The company decided to seek redress from the courts. In the lower court Mr Justice Farwell found for the company, a judgment reversed on appeal. However, in the House of lords the five law Lords agreed unanimously with the view of Lord Halsbury, the Lord Chancellor: 'If the Legislature has created a thing which can own property, which can employ servants, and which can inflict injury, it must be taken, I think, to have impliedly given the power to make it sueable in a Court of Law for injuries purposely done by its authority and procurement.'

The courts had expressly declared against the Taff Vale picketing and had fixed legal liability on the ASRS, enabling the Taff Vale company to secure £23,000 from the union. The importance of the Taff Vale ruling was not immediately understood by the unions. The decision on picketing was reaffirmed in a weavers' strike at Blackburn when the use of persuasion by picketers was ruled illegal and not covered by the Conspiracy and Protection of Property Act 1875 which defined picketing as restricted to 'obtaining and communicating information'. At the TUC in Swansea in 1901 delegates expressed alarm at the re-writing of the 1875 Act, although the Parliamentary Committee had no proposals to hand.

Not all labour sympathisers, not even all unionists were hostile to the Taff Vale decision. Clegg, Fox and Thompson (36) point out that 'Sidney Webb saw Taff Vale as a step towards full corporate status, legally enforceable agreements and compulsory arbitration'. Richard Bell described Taff Vale as 'useful influence' productive of 'wholesome discipline' and one trade union leader at least described picketing as 'an outworn device'. Others saw the hand of the socialists, the wild men, the younger bloods, in the whole affair, and urged a more responsible attitude by responsible union members.

The debate in the House in May 1902 highlighted the precarious position of the unions. On a Liberal motion 'that legislation is necessary to prevent workmen being placed by judge-made law in a position inferior to that intended by Parliament in 1875', the Conservative Government made clear that they could see no case for fresh law. Liberal failure and lukewarmness strengthened the arguments for an independent Labour group in the House. If the Lib-Lab alliance produced so little, then Keir Hardie's remedy should perhaps be given a trial.

THE LRC, THE MINERS AND THE TEXTILE WORKERS

Trade union membership of the LRC had been 232,000 in July 1900, rose to 383,773 by June 1901 and then to 626,613 by May 1902. This dramatic expansion must certainly reflect the impact of Taff Vale. After the debate in the Commons, LRC support increased again to 847,315 by February 1903. However the total number of union members was now 1,942,000 of whom 1,423,000 were affiliated to the TUC so that the LRC still had to capture large sections of the working class for the policy of an independent labour party in Parliament.

Two major unions which had not given their allegiance were the textile workers and the miners. Both these unions were strongly based and both accepted the need for pressure groups within Parliament to influence legislation with industrial implications; initially both were unwilling to think in terms of a party outside the ranks of the two historic parties.

The United Textile Factory Workers' Association, formed in 1886, made one of its main purposes keeping a watchful eye on parliamentary legislation, and James Mawdsley as secretary represented the typical Lancashire working man, Conservative and traditionally hostile to the Liberal Party, the party of his boss. A by-election in Clitheroe offered the occasion for a shift of policy.

There were several special factors operating which helped to bring about this shift to the LRC (43), involving 103,000 textile workers. Both the SDF and the ILP had a foothold in Clitheroe and the voice of socialism had a hearing in *The Socialist Journal*, produced jointly by the two socialist groups. What was fundamental in giving the ILP the edge was that in the two largest towns in the constituency, Nelson and Colne, the Independent Methodists were firmly temperance. Unhappily, on the drink question the SDF were unsound; not so the ILP, who stood solidly behind the Independent Methodists. Again, the Nelson weavers had declared themselves on behalf of a policy of 'returning representatives to Parliament and on all public bodies from our own class'.

Of the 19,400 voters in the constituency, 18,000 were trade unionists. Keir Hardie's tactics to outflank the Liberals were masterly. The Liberals had a candidate ready, but the local ILP put forward a Yorkshire man, Philip Snowden, and then withdrew him to back David Shackleton, a prominent trade unionist, who although basically a Liberal was prepared to accept the new philosophy of independence. The Liberals were reluctant to allow the return of a trade unionist of doubtful loyalty but were finally prevailed upon to do so.

Clitheroe demonstrated the truth underlying the Reform Bills of 1867 and 1884, that the future lay with the working-class voter. Clitheroe could have been as important in the history of the Labour Party as Clare had been in the history of the Catholic Association. It demonstrated that as the majority of voters in most constituencies were working-class, they now had the power to return a working-class majority to the House. At Clitheroe local trade unionists had effectively demanded the seat from the customary tenant. The immediate effect was not a repetition of this *coup d'état* throughout England's working-class constituencies but something more modest, but nevertheless important: the winning over of the textile workers to the LRC and the abandonment of Mawdsley's policy.

For the miners and the MFGB the process was much slower, although their electoral power had been used since 1874. The concentration of miners in mining communities meant that the whole vote could be called out to support their candidate. By 1910 the mining vote made up as much as 10 per cent of the vote (or more) in eighty-six constituencies. This formidable power was wielded on behalf of the Liberals. Ben Pickard, the MFGB President, bitterly opposed the idea that miners' money should be used to send members from other unions to the Commons. This, together with his antipathy to socialism, kept the miners within the Liberal fold.

The miners were affected by Taff Vale, not towards support for LRC, but to Pickard's policy of increasing miners' MPs. Roy Gregory (65) has analysed the elections of 1885 to 1908 to see how the Lib-Lab combination worked out for the miners. Of the twenty-two miners returned in those years, in only eight cases was the miner adopted for a safe Liberal seat. The Liberals were no more generous to their loyal allies than to any other working-class group.

The LRC's spectacular success in 1906 when they won twenty-nine seats brought about a final change of policy. A working-class independent party now clearly existed in the Commons, and by 1908 the miners had affiliated to the LRC. By 1909 the LRC had the support of 1,486,000 trade unionists out of the 1,648,000 affiliated to the TUC.

9 The State and the Worker

Increasingly, in the years before the Great War, the state was to try to deal directly or indirectly with the problems of poverty, sickness and unemployment. Old age pensions, unemployment insurance, employment exchanges and health insurance all underlined the growing willingness of the state to accept responsibility for the social difficulties of its citizens. Socialist members of trade unions had campaigned in the last twenty years of the nineteenth century for positive state action, none more vigorously than in the field of unemployment. In 1886 Tom Mann, in his pamphlet on the Eight Hour Day had argued that a compulsory eight hour day would provide employment for 750,000 extra workers. Keir Hardie in 1887 had declared that 'there are one million strong able-bodied men out of work today for whom the passing of an Eight Hours Bill would find employment'.

Fundamental to the debate within the unions on the eight-hour day (in 1887 the TUC spent two days debating the issue) was what A.E.P. Duffy has called 'the positive desire to enrol the aid of the state'. Voluntaryism, traditional to both sides of industry, could no longer deal with the problem of mass unemployment. The eight-hour movement gathered force and won the support of the gasworkers and the miners and by 1889 the carpenters, the railway servants, iron founders, the stonemasons, and the compositors had all committed themselves. In 1890 when the conservative textile workers gave their support, the TUC voted by 132 votes to 21 in favour of state action to limit the working day to eight hours. However in giving evidence to the Royal Commission socialist trade unionists apart from Will Thorne played down the virtues of the legal eight-hour day as the answer to unemployment because of evidence in industry, particularly in engineering, where the eight-hour day had been tried, that production did not fall but remained constant despite the reduction in the work day. That the state should take some action was still essential, but it was no longer quite so obvious what form that action should take.

With unemployment, poverty must rank as the major two social tragedies of pre-war England. The study Seebohm Rowntree had made of York in 1899 (39) painted a disturbing picture of the realities of working class life. More than 40 per cent of town workers lived in poverty, defined by Rowntree as the lack of means to secure 'the minimum of food, clothing, and shelter needful for the maintenance of merely physical health'. At that level of existence there was never enough money to buy newspapers, write letters, join a sick club or buy attractive clothes for the children. It was essential that the wage-earner should never stay away from work, even for one day, for this would plunge the family even further down the scale. Similar studies in other towns such as Northampton and Reading, undertaken in 1912 and 1913, confirmed these findings.

The Edwardian years were a period in which poverty did not appreciably diminish: they were also a time of troubles in the trade unions, a phase of rapid expansion of membership and the growth of militancy. Many reasons may be found to suggest why trade unions were more prone to strike action than before, of which the attempted comprehensiveness of the mass unions would be one, but the background to discontent was the changing pattern of prices and unchanging pattern of wages. In the last decades of the nineteenth century the English working man had steadily improved his economic position; for the average worker wages had not risen but prices had dropped so that, as E.H. Phelps Brown points out, 'the basketful of goods that the average British wage would buy had increased by two-thirds' in the last thirty years (57). Built into normal expectations was the assumption that this pattern of life would continue into the future. However in the years before 1914 this expectation did not hold good and working men looked for explanations in the arguments put forward by socialists and by the advocates of that syndicalism so strong in France, in Italy, in Spain and to some extent in the United States.

An increasingly adverse movement of the terms of world trade had affected domestic prices at a time when the speed of technical advance which had earlier been so beneficial to Britain was slowing up. If there was no rapid increase in the amount of products which manufacturing Britain had to exchange, if output per man remained constant rather than increased, adverse terms of trade would soon be reflected in the higher prices which British shoppers would have to pay. It is no coincidence that this period was also the time when Joseph Chamberlain was advancing ideas on how to offset the effect on Britain of the impact of new technologies in Germany and America. Again a falling off of demand in the export markets both produced alarmingly deep pockets of unemployment in the export industries and had consequential effects on construction of various kinds, notably in shipbuilding and domestic building. In some of these trades unemployment would rise as high as 20 per cent against a national average of 9 per cent. Particularly bad years were 1908 and 1909. The sense of bitter hopelessness and the conviction that remedies must be found were the background for these tragic years.

Faced by the clear evidence of the extent of the problem produced by the Royal Commission on the Poor Law, the Liberal government constructed new social services; the Old Age Pensions Act of 1908, the National Insurance and Unemployment Acts of 1911, aimed at allaying the distress and starvation produced by ill health and unemployment among the working class. All these measures were a new and significant recognition of social responsibility and Flora Thompson in *Lark Rise to Candleford* has described the sense of wonder and gratitude that the aged poor of Candleford felt in receiving their free old age pensions.

The Liberals also extended radically the scope of the existing legislation on industrial injury and workmen's compensation. The history of the attempts to create a satisfactory framework for compensation reached well back into the late nineteenth century. Certain occupations such as mining, or any occupation involving physical skills such as road or bridge building, or connected with moving machinery such as on the railways, were recognised as notoriously dangerous. Death in the mines or on the railways was a commonplace of Victorian life. Against such dangers the craft unions had built up friendly society reserves but these were not large enough to offer that lifelong support which disablement might require.

Within the context of the self-help state, there was no remedy for this. However as the political philosophy underlying the state began slowly to change trade unionists began to press for state action to protect the employee. Since 1872 the TUC Parliamentary Committee had had an Employers' Liability Bill in their programme, and in 1873 the Gladstone government had promised legislation. In 1875 the miners' MP Alexander MacDonald had put his own Bill to the Commons and the Disraeli government had responded by setting up a select committee of inquiry.

The central problem was the doctrine of common employment which held that if the injured person was in common employment with the person committing the injury, the employer would not be negligible. Macdonald's Bill had firmly rejected this doctrine, but the Tory Parliament only softened its impact by admitting the responsibility of the manager.

With the return of the Liberals in 1880 a more generous measure was introduced, but the doctrine of common employment still stood. However, the need for employers to insure their workmen against injury was recognised. This law formally allowed employers to contract out of their responsibilities under the Common Law. If employer and employees could reach agreement in setting up a fund to which both subscribed, the employee could then voluntarily abandon his Common Law rights. Contracting out became established practice in some areas of the coal industry and in rail companies such as the London and Brighton and the London and North Western.

For the next sixteen years the TUC and its Parliamentary Committee sought to have the concept of employers' liability widened to end the practice of contracting out and to remove the doctrine of common employment which so gravely restricted the rights of employees to claim compensation for injuries at work. In 1893 Gladstone agreed to end contracting out and to close the loopholes provided by the doctrine of common employment. A new Employers' Liability Bill was passed through the Commons but was disastrously mutilated in the Lords. It was left to Joseph Chamberlain in the Salisbury Government in 1897 to produce a Workmen's Compensation Bill which compelled employers to insure workers against accidents. Certain major groups of workers were excluded from the Bill — agricultural workers and merchant seamen in particular — but in 1903 the Tory government added landworkers.

The Liberal extension of the Act in 1906 brought in another six million workers and broke new ground by including industrial diseases such as anthrax and lead poisoning. Initially only six diseases were included but within the year the government added another eighteen. The one great drawback of the measure was that it did not compel employers to insure against the costs of paying compensation, so that for the injured workman there was no guarantee his employer would have sufficient funds to meet his claim. However this series of Acts had helped to create a buffer, no matter how limited, against the hazards of industrial employment.

The TUC's Parliamentary Committee campaigned actively for old age pensions, beginning in 1906 with a deputation to the new Liberal government and following up with countrywide public meetings. In 1907, with nothing yet introduced into the Commons, Congress passed a resolution deploring the lack of progress and then held a further series of protest meetings calling for immediate legislation. No government could afford lightly to ignore the working-class voter or an organisation with 1¾ million supporters, and Lloyd George in 1908 brought in a Bill to provide non-contributory old age pensions.

For similar reasons, the Balfour Government in 1903 had appointed a Royal Commission to look at the legal position of the trade unions in the aftermath of Taff Vale. The Commission was boycotted by the unions, and when its report was published in 1906 the Liberal landslide had created a new political situation in the House. There were twenty-nine LRC MPs, fourteen miners' MPs (not associated with the LRC until 1909) and more than a dozen Lib-Labs. The Commission's report went far to meet the objections of trade unionists. Peaceful persuasion was to be allowed, and the legalisation given to acts in combination permitted by the 1875 legislation was to be maintained. Where the proposals fell far short of trade union expectations was on the sensitive issue of protection of funds. Here unions were only to be actionable as civil law if the damages to a company resulted from officially endorsed action by the trade unions concerned.

The Liberals introduced a Bill along the lines of the Commission's report but immediately found itself under fire in the House from Labour MPs, from Liberals, and from some Conservatives. The government acted promptly, redrafted the Bill to give unions complete protection for their funds and to allow union members to picket. Outside the House, employers viewed the new Bill with great hostility, for it seemed to place trade unions in a uniquely privileged position, and, in their view, such undue protection might encourage unnecessary strikes (68).

The judiciary's power to alter fundamentally the position of trade unions was once more demonstrated in the famous Osborne judgment (1909). Osborne, a railwayman and a Liberal, tried unsuccessfully to persuade his own union, the ASRS, to abandon the practice by which union funds supported the Labour Party. Osborne, with the free legal advice of antisocialist solicitors, decided to test the legality of this practice in the courts, with funds from his own union. In the lower court, the courts upheld the legality of the subsidy but the Court of Appeal ruled against it. The railway union then took the case to the House of Lords, where all five Law Lords supported the Court of Appeal's decision. The Lords used the analogy of the joint stock company and laid down that the trade union Acts did not specifically give power to the unions to raise a political levy. This levy must consequently be illegal, a ruling which would make illegal many other trade union activities ranging from education to running a newspaper.

The Labour Party tried to have the judgment reversed in the Commons and saw the whole affair as evidence of a capitalist plot to destroy the Party. The judgment did not prove as immediately disastrous as the labour Party feared. The new MP's salary of £400 a year, first introduced in 1911, softened the blow, and many expedients were devised to help trade unionist MPs in the post-Osborne world. The aids ranged from voluntary political funds within the union, which was not very productive, to help from the central funds of the Labour Party which were expanded by public subscription.

Osborne was partly overturned in 1913 when the Liberals introduced a Bill which permitted members to contract out if they did not wish to pay a political levy. The Labour Party was not happy with this for they wished to have Osborne completely reversed, but after a long struggle they accepted the measure as the best available.

10   A Time of Troubles

In the years preceding the First World War, institutionalised procedures for dealing with grievances and potential conflicts grew very rapidly. In 1894 there were sixty-four conciliation and arbitration boards; by 1913 there were 325. The means of preserving industrial peace had grown rapidly within the organised sector of British industry, where collective bargaining was the norm and trade unions had been recognised. Within any one year the number of working days lost by industrial disputes ranged between one million to four million in 1901, an exceptional year, with most years well below three million. In the years from 1910 to 1914 this pattern was radically changed, with days lost around the ten million mark except in 1912 when there were nearly forty-one million. Were there any special factors operating in the last years before the outbreak of 1914-18 war which account for this intensification of industrial conflict?

One common cause is easily identified: the years 1909 to 1913 saw a rapid expansion in trade and industry and therefore a time of rising expectations for trade unionists. Again, of the three major industries affected, the mines, the railways and the docks, only one, mining, had the benefits of established procedures and employers' recognition, and here a specific problem, that of 'abnormal places', broadened into a demand for state protection through a minimum wage. Furthermore, the reappearance of full employment strengthened those general unions created in the expansion of 1889-92 which had managed to survive. During these years before the war the Workers' Union made its most spectacular gains, growing from 4,500 in 1910 to 143,000 in 1914 and carried through a series of successful strikes such as those in the Black Country in 1913. These strikes had traditional union objectives: the achievement of a 23 shillings weekly minimum for men and 12 shillings for women.

The vote had brought no obvious and immediate gains in the standard of life of the working classes and they sought to strengthen their economic defences by trade union organisation; membership rose between 1900 and 1914 from two million to well over four million, with the major increase taking place in the final four years, from 2½ to 4 million. In 1910 trade unions covered only 17 per cent of the working population and for these workers (apart from the railwaymen, who still had no recognition) there were at least established collective bargaining procedures which offered some protection against rising prices. Outside this small sector of British industry, there was no protection whatsoever.

How far was new militancy part of that apparently general breakdown in British institutions symbolised by the constitutional crisis, Conservative irresponsibility towards Ulster, the new stridency in the suffragettes' campaign? (53) Perhaps very little indeed, for good alternative explanations can be found for the increasing industrial discontent in the immediate pre-war years. Amongst these the failure of normal expectations might rank very large, and to some extent the development of an economic analysis of present discontents. Industrial workers found in Marx not only an analysis of the historic growth of capitalism but a prophecy of the way in which a post-capitalist society could be brought into being. Again that dissatisfaction with parliamentary politics and reformism which in Spain had stimulated the growth of anarcho-syndicalism, produced in England an interest in nationwide syndicates which would eventually take over British industry.

The key figure here was Tom Mann (6) who in his memoirs, explains how his knowledge of French trade unionism radically altered his ideas on trade union policy. 'I declared myself', he writes' definitely in favour of industrial unionism and direct action as the main channel for the outflow of our activities.' The French trade union organisation, the *Confédération Générale du Travail* he admired as the powerhouse of ideas which would transform capitalist society into socialist society. In *The Industrial Syndicalist's* first issue in 1910 he proclaimed that a syndicalist movement must be 'avowedly and clearly revolutionary in aim and method'. He saw this as a refusal to enter into long-term agreements and a willingness to use every opportunity which presented itself for a fight. Such techniques would lead on inevitably to a socialist society.

Emmet Larkin in his biography of the Irish labour leader, James Larkin (5) has shown that a major source for British syndicalism was the American syndicalist organisation, the Industrial Workers of the World, which emphasised the need for a centralised industrial union as opposed to the French and Spanish emphasis on localism.

In Britain syndicalist ideas took firmest root in South Wales where in 1912 the publication of *The Miners' Next Step* opened up the argument for a union takeover of industry and the eventual formation of a syndicalist democracy. The pamphlet was financed by the South Wales Miners' Federation and the syndicalist arguments found a ready audience amongst leading members of the miners' union. [doc. 17].

The writer called for the formation of a single industrywide union and the amalgamation movement reflects these new ideas. The creation of the National Union of Railwaymen in 1913 from the Amalgamated Society of Railway Servants, the General Railway Workers' Union and the United Signalmen and Pointsmen's Society looked like a major step towards this goal, although ASLEF and the Railway Clerks refused to join. A similar move in transport was made by Tom Mann himself, with the help of his old comrade-in-arms, Ben Tillett, secretary of the Dockers' Union, who campaigned for an all-inclusive transport union (excluding the railwaymen); this produced the National Transport Workers' Federation in 1910, which took in the National Sailors' and Firemen's union.

In Ireland, James Larkin campaigned for 'One Big Union', comprising a militant and aggressive working class, and his Irish Transport Workers' Union approached more nearly the syndicalist model that any other trade union in Great Britain. Larkin, as Emmet Larkin observes, 'saw society in three stages – the present, the near future, and the millennium' (5). As the millenium must necessarily be some distance away, Larkin's 'One Big Union' tended to have immediate and practical objectives, among which were the establishment of Wages Boards to regulate wages in different industries. The need for union organisation was obvious and the differences in the standard of life of the English and Irish worker most profound. One of Larkin's early successes was bringing the farm labourers of County Dublin into his Transport Union. Agricultural wages in Ireland were roughly two-thirds of those in England (11s3d to 18s4d per week), and Larkin organised a pre-harvest strike which brought them up almost to English standards. He advocated the sympathetic strike, and his great battle, lasting eight months, with the Dublin employers in 1913 foundered partly because he was unable to bring out the TUC in support. It was a major setback for Irish trade unionism and it was fought on both sides with a ferocity normally absent from British industrial disputes.

It is easy to overstate the influence of these new ideas, yet what gave edge to the new militancy was the accumulating evidence of the great social and economic divisions in English society, evidence not only from Royal Commissions, but from Charles Booth, from the new realistic novels of H.G. Wells and the writings of socialists like Robert Blatchford. The strikes which took place arose from diverse causes: the railwaymen for recognition, the miners for a minimum wage, the dockers and seamen for an increase in wages. To middle-class England they seemed to harbinger a slide towards the total disintegration of English society, all produced by one general cause; yet strikes were industrial rather than political, aimed at specific objectives which, once achieved, produced stability and industrial peace.

One other symptom of the working-class discontent of the times was reflected in the growth of rank and file militancy in the unions, partly perhaps a distrust of official procedures which always worked too slowly, partly a generalised anger with the levels of working-class life. Even the great traditional societies such as the ASE were not immune, and in 1912 a delegate meeting threw out all the members of the Executive Council, who then barricaded themselves in their head-quarters in Peckham Road. This unseemly affair first ended with an invasion from the house next door and was finally closed in the courts.

The new responsibility assumed by the state, explicitly assumed in the welfare legislation, also appeared in the direct intervention of the central government in two major disputes, in mining and in rail transport, and in the growth of support services to achieve industrial peace. The government had assumed a role in industrial policy through the 1896 Conciliation Act, largely made effective through the devoted and diplomatic work of G.R. Askwith (67), the Board of Trade's great trouble-shooter, who was regarded by both sides in industry as above the battle. An abortive attempt was made to extend the role of the state as a conciliator by the creation in 1911 of the Industrial Council, with Askwith as its Chairman. The Council was the brainchild of Sir Charles Macara, a Manchester cotton magnate, who proposed a ministry responsible for labour affairs as part of his overall plan for industrial harmony. From the beginning the Council had no teeth, it had no power to intervene and could only act when invited to do so. It lasted for only two years and during its short life was largely ignored by the government. Rodger Charles (60) makes the point that the government never took it seriously although it attracted some distinguished trade unionists to serve: Thomas Burt of the Miners, Harry Gosling of the National Transport Workers' Federation, J.R. Clynes of the Gas-workers, and Arthur Henderson of the Ironfounders. In his view the Council was set up on the false assumption that 'national conciliation could help to remove the cause of industrial unrest — mass poverty and the refusal of wage earners at the lower end of the scale to tolerate it any longer.' [doc. 19] .

If the perennial trade union concern lay behind the industrial disturbances of the time, could the creation of the Triple Industrial Alliance in 1914 be seen as a more revolutionary step, an abandonment of traditional trade union objectives? George Dangerfield (53) so read this event: 'clear evidence of the coming major conflict between Capital and Labour, the great General Strike of 1914, luckily forestalled by some bullets at Sarajevo'. In his view had this General Strike coincided with civil war in Ireland, England could well have undergone a revolution.

This highly dramatic account rests on a misunderstanding of the purpose of the Triple Industrial Alliance. The Alliance rested upon the Miners' Federation (870,000 members) together with the NUR (268,000) and the NTWF (163,000) by which they pledged common action. The constitution made no specific provision for sympathetic strikes nor even a commitment to try to secure a common date for renegotiation of wage agreements so as to use their combined industrial power to get the best wage deals for their members, an idea strongly put forward by Will Thorne of the NTWF.

P.S. Bagwell (87) observes that 'only a small minority of the leaders ever considered that the purpose of the alliance was to bring about revolutionary change'. 'It is clear', says John Lovell (59) 'that the intention of the founders of the Alliance was not to maximise industrial conflict, let alone precipitate a revolutionary crisis on syndicalist lines'. G.A. Phillips (88) makes the point even more strongly – 'To many of its founders indeed it was welcomed as a means of averting stoppages, not as a means of enlarging them.' Indeed 'they welcomed it as a symbol of, and support for, the principle of amalgamation and organisation by industry.' British Trade Unions, before the First World War, did not plan a great leap forward into a revolutionary future but were attempting, not very coherently, to make existing industrial practices more effective.

Strikes, hard bargaining, struggles for improvement took place in many industries between 1910 and 1914, and all three major industries, mines, railways, docks were affected in turn. In mining the struggle began over that longstanding problem, 'abnormal places'. In many pits this problem was got over by 'a consideration', a customary extra payment to men working on very hard and difficult seams. However the close involvement of Conciliation Boards in the industry with a stricter supervision of rates had led many larger companies to cut down or even cut out the 'con'. In 1910 the Miners' Federation in Conference had called for 'a living wage to be paid to all miners working in abnormal places'.

It was just such a problem which began the struggle in the Rhondda valley in 1910 between the miners at the Ely pit, and the Cambrian Collieries, the pit's owners. The mineowners opened the battle by locking out the miners at Ely, not only the seventy men who refused the proposed rate for a very difficult seam, but the whole mining community at Ely pit, all 800 men. The South Wales Miners' Federation responded by calling out the 12,000 miners working for Cambrian with the declared policy of teaching 'that particular company that tyrannical action over certain men to influence others was not a paying policy'. The Aberdare Valley followed the Cambrian miners and soon 30,000 men were idle.

At Tonypandy the threat of blackleg labour brought a brush between strikers and police. The Chief Constable of Glamorgan telephoned the Home Secretary, Winston Churchill, for troop support. Churchill appointed General Macready to command both the civil and military forces in the area. On 21 November 1910 at Tonypandy Macready reported the use of 'small bodies of infantry' who 'by a little gentle persuasion with the bayonet drove the stone-throwers into the arms of the police' [doc. 18], an unprecedented use of armed force in a civil dispute.

The Cambrian strike lasted well into the autumn of 1911, when finally the miners were forced back on the owners' terms. At the local level, the strike was a failure, yet nationally it pushed the problem of abnormal places to the forefront of mining politics. The next step forward was the minimum wage issue. A special conference, called in November 1911 in London, considered in full the question of a national minimum, which would resolve the thorny problem of abnormal places. The NFGB proposed a meeting with the owners to negotiate a settlement. When the owners rejected a meeting, the mining union balloted its members on a national strike over this single issue. More than two-thirds of the miners voted for direct action and the miners' executive fixed a date in February 1912 for a national miner's strike.

The Prime Minister threw his weight — and that of the government — into the scale and summoned the whole 170 MFGB delebates to a meeting. Government policy was to try to reach agreement that minimum wages should be by district and in return for government support for this principle the miners should abandon their demand for a national minimum. The miners stood firm and a minority of coal owners would not accept the halfway house of the government's plan. On 1 March 1912 the national coal strike began and nearly a million men came out.

To make clear the strength of government support for the policy of a local minimum wage the Liberals hurriedly passed the Coal Mines Minimum Wages Act, which gave statutory force to their policy. The mine owners then capitulated and the miners took another ballot of members which produced only a small majority in favour of continuing the strike. The Executive accepted the view that as two thirds were needed to bring the miners out on strike, two-thirds majority was necessary to continue the strike and consequently called the men back to work.

The strike had lasted six weeks and had involved more workers than any previous strike. As R. Page Arnot points out (16) it ended with great dissatisfaction amongst the pitmen, who felt that the government had cheated them of 'an assured victory'. But it had achieved effective safeguards for the miners in abnormal places. Wage scales were to be local; the Minimum Wage Boards could not impose settlements. The basic district wage was fixed by collective bargaining and all that the local board could do was to ensure that the negotiated wage was paid.

The struggle on the railways arose from the failure of the unions to secure recognition by their employers, by now a continuing provocation even to moderates like Richard Bell, the Amalgamated Society's secretary. In 1907 Bell fired the opening shot in a major campaign for recognition by demanding a shorter day and a guaranteed working week. The traditional craft union, ASLEF, took a similar line. All the railway companies, except the North Eastern, refused to negotiate and a strike ballot produced 77,000 (out of 88,000) in favour of immediate strike action. Fearing the effect on the nation's economy of a protracted struggle, Lloyd George, President of the Board of Trade, intervened. He threatened the companies with a statute making arbitration compulsory in rail disputes; reluctantly, they gave way and opened negotiations. Recognition was discussed, only to be rejected, and the companies came forward with a complicated scheme of conciliation boards for the industry. The 1907 conciliation scheme achieved little for the railway unions, partly because each company negotiated separately and no general decisions could be reached binding on rail companies as a whole.

The 1907 plan was intended to run for seven years but survived only to 1911 when feeling ran so high amongst the rank and file that an unofficial strike at Liverpool triggered off a series of others. The four rail unions met and called for a national strike on 17 August unless the rail companies would meet for negotiations. Not unexpectedly the railway companies followed their traditional policy of refusing to negotiate with the rail unions and the strike followed with a massive withdrawal of labour, crippling a good deal of the normal rail traffic.

The government intervened, promising a Royal Commission of Inquiry, thereby effectively drawing steam from the protest and the railway unions called for a return to work. The subsequent report failed to conciliate the unions and they once more demanded negotiations direct with the companies, with an open threat of a renewed strike if the companies persisted in refusing. Once more the government stepped in as a middle-man and called a meeting, with G.R. Askwith in the chair. This round of negotiations got the unions what they wanted. As Askwith said: 'For good or evil, practical recognition of the unions, and the principle of negotiation with the railway companies as a body were the chief results of the railway strike of 1911'. Askwith records a new theme in Lloyd George's interview with the railway directors, an appeal to the national interest, a reference to the 'national danger'. It was the time of the Moroccan crisis, when Germany had sent the gunboat Panther to Morocco to uphold her alleged business interests at Agadir, and the argument necessarily prevailed with the railway authorities when put by the government (67).

The 1911 Conciliation Scheme, with its implicit recognition of railway trade unionism, was a clear victory for militancy, and gave an enormous fillip to the railway unions. From 116,000 in 1911 the total membership rose to 184,000 by the end of 1912; by 1914 it had risen to 337,000, making railway trade unionism one of the great powers of the trade union world.

Dockers, like railwaymen, suffered from lack of recognition, and in 1911 the expanded NTWF supported the seamen's struggle with the Shipping Federation by calling on the dock employers to grant recognition and a standard port rate. The Devonport agreement brought this period of unrest to an end with new pay scales, but without conceding recognition. The NTWF submitted this newly won agreement to a mass meeting and suffered the humiliation of rejection. Individual sections began to down tools, with union leaders desperately trying to restrain them. Finally the leadership had to reject the new Devonport agreement and in August the employers made further substantial concessions. Thus 1911 was a year of victory for the dockers: although they had not secured recognition they had secured major wage improvements.

In 1912 the success of the miners, argues John Lovell (21), encouraged the dockers when they began a battle with the newly constituted Port of London Authority, chaired by Lord Devonport, to demand the exclusion of non-unionists, and implicitly to gain union recognition. The NTWF called a national strike but they did not have behind them the disciplined ranks of the miners' unions and the strike call went largely unanswered, except in Bristol (8). The traditional localism of the dockers reasserted itself and the London dockers found themselves leading a phantom army. The NTWF was defeated and began to wither away, with employers triumphantly returning to the pre-1911 methods of hiring. Only the stevedores remained as a dock force with some bargaining power based on employer recognition, and in the provinces Bristol was to become the power behind the future organisation of dockland's power.

Although the dockers' union did not readily expand, the overall picture of trade union growth is impressive. In 1909 total membership stood at 2,477,000; in 1910 it was 2,565,000. This was the point of take-off with membership rising to 3,139,000 in 1911. By 1914 there were 4,145,000 trade union members, a remarkably firm base for the great expansion of the war years which was to bring membership by 1920 up to double that figure.

PART THREE

Assessment

Assessment

Since the Napoleonic wars a new Britain had developed, a Britain no longer basically agrarian and ruled by county grandees within an archaic political framework but a Britain dependent on a flourishing industry and with a complex social hierarchy. A diversifying middle class ran from bankers through industrialists and an increasing civil service down to the state school teacher. Into that social structure fitted the new trade union leader, belonging to the middling classes, often, like George Howell, personally ambitious to join the governing classes. Into that industrial framework slotted the trade union which by 1914 had in some industries such as engineering or mining become the established and accepted representative of the workers in that industry.

Such a change was slow to achieve and might be seen as paralleled by or analogous to the democratisation of the franchise which had taken place politically. Working men now had political power, with their own small party in the Commons including spokesmen with trade union backgrounds such as Keir Hardie or John Burns, and they had industrial organisations which bargained with employers for the maintenance or improvement of the standard of living. It would be easy to exaggerate this change, after all by 1914 only slightly more than one in four were trade unionists, but the pattern had been set, and was increasingly to be followed in industries relatively unaffected by unionism. In the absence of any systematic regulations of wages by the state, the trade union was the only means by which questions of pay and conditions could be negotiated within industry. The smaller the industry, the less susceptible to trade unionisation it could be; the sweat shops of the East End had to be dealt with by the state in the Trade Boards Act 1909. The larger the industry the more effectively it could be organised. Yet the potential for unionisation in a large industry would depend on other factors, the level of pay; which would in turn affect the possibility of collecting trade union dues; or the extent of casual labour; or the incidence of unemployment. The union had been most effective in large industries with a good employment record. In a small industry with scattered and small sites, the work force could only be effectively unionised if a high level of skill was needed.

Trade unions had developed from trade societies and had traditionally been concerned with protecting the interests of their members and providing a limited number of benefits, of which the most basic was funeral benefit. Again, trade unions had been traditionally exclusive in trying to restrict membership to those who had been through the appropriate apprenticeship, and in trying to maintain the family connection so that the next generation of workers would be the sons of existing members. The concept of the closed shop or a hereditary aristocracy could be seen at work even in the early trade societies. Their other main characteristic was that they had been local. The change from local to national society began with the Amalgamated Society of Engineers in 1851. By 1914 most trade unions were national rather than local, although in some industries, notably mining and weaving, strongly local unions were banded together into federations. Again the concept of national rather than local carried with it to some extent the idea of a London headquarters, although by 1914 this was not universal. A London headquarters made parliamentary pressure easier to organise but many industries were basically regional, with no roots in London at all. The disadvantages of too strong a London bias had been shown in the early days of the TUC when provincial unions were clearly resenting the supremacy which the London 'Junta' assumed to itself.

Trade unions, too, had changed radically both in size and in structure. The old craft unions had steadily grown – the ASE with 10,800 in 1851 had 170,000 in 1914 - and similar increases had taken place in other unions of craft workers. Some New Unions such as the Workers' Union, had grown even more spectacularly. The overall increase was reflected in the number of trade unionists affiliated to the TUC, which had rocketed from just over a million in 1893 to over two and a half million in 1914. The actual number of trade unions had slightly declined, from 1,279 to 1,260, in the same period. The change in structure was most marked in the rapid increase in the number of permanent officials. The first permanent official had been appointed by the Old Mechanics in the 1840s; by 1914 all unions had their permanent officials at the centre, and in some cases district organisers.

The development of a permanent structure had not been without problems. The Junta unions had been anxious to control strike activity through the Executive Council, so that any strike would be official and have full union backing. The growing power of the Executive Council in all unions had created resentments at branch level in the face of grass-roots trade unionism. The appearance of the shop steward has set up a spokesman for this grassroots movement who increasingly came to see his role as that of the true representative of the men on the spot against the bureaucracy of the Executive Council and the permanent officials. The shop steward was the counterpart of the checkweighman in the mining industry or the father of the chapel in the printing industry and marks a partial return of that localism from which British trade unionism developed. As an official he arises from the work group itself and Clegg, Fox and Thompson (36), point out 'that by 1897 the employers' leader complained that in every shop and in every department there have been for years, what are known as shop stewards, members of the ASE, whose duty it is to see that the rules are carried out, and he is a brave employer who dares to say nay to their demands'. The shop steward was to speak for 'rank and file' unionism and to claim with some justice to understand work problems more intimately than men who had been promoted into administration as salaried officials. In unions like the ASE it was the shop steward who could obstruct assimilating policies directed towards expanding the union by taking in the less highly skilled, for the shop steward could speak with accepted authority on the ordinary member's need to preserve wage differentials which craft union membership had built up.

For the permanent officials experience of negotiation with employers, and occasional contact with the higher reaches of the civil service and ministers not only sharpened their powers but often gave them a taste for politics. The way forward was seen to be through the Commons to high rank in the Liberal Party, and later in the Labour Party. Trade union officials were courted by MPs, by Fabians, by any group concerned with working-class life. As MPs they were given an independent income and faced the danger of assimilation into the existing class structure and an abandonment of working-class life and possibly trade union interests. Membership of this new group could lead to a capacity for an overview which might make it difficult to see the standpoint of trade unionists themselves.

In the period which this book covers, the fundamental relationship of the trade unions themselves to society had been transformed. In 1825 trade unions had just secured a lifting of legal sanctions; by 1914 they were strong enough to secure through their own party and through influence in the Liberal Party a change in law itself, the 1911 Trade Union Act. The unions had ceased to be bodies which would be legislated for or against, they had become bodies with the ability to secure legislation on their own behalf, either through the political parties or through the technique of lobbying, so sedulously pursued by the TUC's Parliamentary Committee.

Nowhere was their changed status more clearly shown than in the conciliation and arbitration processes which had grown up. Union representatives became the 'real respectability'; they sat with employers on conciliation boards; they shared Liberal platforms with employers. Their activities could well be seen as the industrial counterpart of the Lib-Lab alliance which existed in politics and in the House of Commons. Many labour historians have been extremely critical of trade union participation in conciliation machinery, criticism which relates to the Webbs and the traditional definition of a trade union. 'A trade union', the Webbs observe, 'as we understand the term, is a continuous association of wage earners for the purpose of improving their conditions of employment'. On this view trade unions that became involved in conciliation processes did not satisfactorily fulfil this function as J.H. Porter has shown (94). In his analysis of conciliation agreements between 1860 and 1914 he concludes that 'whilst it is true that advances were made, these were less than might otherwise have been obtained'. Furthermore he suggests that 'the restrictive nature of the agreements was increasingly realised by the rank and file as the rising prices eroded their standard of living'. He makes one other fundamental criticism concerning the rise and fall of prices where wage agreements have both a built-in minimum and maximum. 'The maximum' he argues,' was far more important as a restrictive factor upon trade unions in times of prosperity than in depression'. In Porter's view the whole system of conciliation procedures retarded the prosperity of trade unionists affected by it. The result was clear in the pre-1914 industrial scene: 'The more militant leaders and rank and file . . . realised that the situation had changed and . . . wished to make full use of their bargaining power by abolishing the conciliation system with its emphasis on moderation and gradual advance.'

V.L. Allen (106) sees the whole process as inhibiting and blunting the growth of trade unions and he is particularly critical of the way in which only the selling price was allowed as the context in which wage settlements were made with no evidence allowed on the cost of living, changes in the level of profits or cost of production.

A definition offered by A.F. Flanders (50) provides a differing critical tool. He sees trade unions 'as a form of organisation which enabled employees . . . to regulate and thus improve their wages and working conditions'. The process of regulating may necessarily involve participation in discussions with management. At what point does discussion with management in a collective bargaining situation endanger the independence of the union involved? does this activity become radically different if carried on within a conciliation council? One clear danger arises if the council on the workers' side is made up of representatives of the workforces rather than trade union representatives, and this double loyalty may make for a conflict of loyalties.

Trade unions in conciliation procedures, just as unionists who work with governments, may find themselves increasingly identified as 'company' men; officials may find themselves alienated from the rank and file. The union may consequently lose control of some of its members, or breakaway unions with a more militant policy will emerge. What may be true is that conciliation machinery will function well when industry is prosperous and allows wages to grow, albeit too slowly, but in a period of industrial depression or of rapidly rising prices the machinery will begin to look too cumbersome, or insufficiently protective of trade union interests.

One major trade union concern was directed towards a limitation of the working day and control of the shape of the working week. After a successful campaign for the Ten-Hour Day in 1844, supported by Shaftesbury in Parliament, and a series of short-time committees in the country, some trade unionists, notably the builders, further sought to limit the working day to nine hours and the builders' lockout of 1851-52 had this as its main objective. The argument turns not only on the need for civilised leisure and the need to lighten the general work load but also on reduction in agreed hours as a means of creating more vacancies for unemployed craftsmen.

A further attempt was made in 1872 when a Bill intended, like its predecessors, to limit the hours of women and children to nine hours, was introduced into the Commons. It had another run in 1873 but without support from a Liberal government susceptible to the hostile comments of the employers. In the general election of 1874 the trade union lobby pressed their proposals on all candidates and with the Conservatives in office the new government introduced their own Bill, which if it did not grant a nine-hour day, did establish as law a 56½-hour week disguised as the Factories (Health of Women) Bill.

Within ten years a new demand was presented for an eight-hour day. The initiative came first from the socialists, mainly supporters of the Social Democratic Federation who had begun their campaign in 1884. With the reappearance of industrial depression in the 1880s the campaign gained a great deal of support, and the TUC asked the Parliamentary Committee to carry out a plebiscite on the question. In the event two plebiscites were carried out, paradoxically by two known opponents, and the results were so difficult to assess that the TUC abandoned the whole matter.

For many trade unionists the issue was far from clearcut, but pressure from the new unions and the miners brought Congress to a vote in favour. In 1891 this proposal was modified to allow particular trades where there was a majority in opposition to opt out. Within two years, however, the option was dropped and Congress then passed an eight hour resolution annually without much opposition or even debate. Increasingly, too, trade unionists lost faith in a limitation of hours as the most effective way of dealing with the social problems of contemporary Britain. Unions began to follow their own paths: the Railwaymen secured a legal limitation of hours in 1893, the Miners won an eight hour day in 1908, but for most workers the legal maximum of eight hours had to wait until a general limitation of hours in 1919 **(96)**.

In the main during the period the unions had seen their role as primarily a role within industry: to protect their standard of living, to control conditions of entry, to secure free collective bargaining, to achieve recognition. Excursions outside this role had had a limited objective, apart from trade union involvement in Chartism, and here the evidence is that it was the weaker or declining unions who became committed to the movement; the more firmly established unions stood aloof or were occasionally to be seen supporting a call for much-needed legislation such as a shorter working week. When trade unions took up a political role at other times it was to promote trade union objectives; to work for electoral reform in the 1860s, or to campaign for working men in Parliament after the Reform Bill of 1867, so that the distinctive voice speaking for working class interests could be heard. Even the formation of the LRC owes more to the reluctance of the Liberals to allow sufficient representation of working men than to a transformation of the trade union movement as a whole to socialism, and initially the LRC and subsequently the Labour Party behaved more like an extension of the Liberal Party than a newly independent socialist party.

This cautious and moderate line in some views lost unions the opportunity to be a revolutionary force in politics. The opportunity arose most clearly in the development of syndicalist views among trade unions affected by continental example and by Tom Mann. Syndicalism through the revolutionary general strike would transform property relations and consequently society. In France and in Spain these ideas had taken firm root, and syndicalism has an attractively messianic quality which appealed to workers whose conditions were depressingly low. Yet in Britain these ideas, although discussed and in the slightly different form of guild socialism with a great appeal to the intellectual left, had very little following. It can be argued that even in the very troubled times of the last four years before the First World War the history of the trade union movement if read right would suggest that improvement, legal, political and industrial, had been secured within the established customs and institutions of society.

The waves of strike indicated a lost confidence in the new industrial procedures, a protest against the bureaucratic slowness of many, a bitter comment on a society which had failed to protect the standard of living. They did not go beyond this to suggest that the next stage would be revolution.

Trade unionists involvement in political activity was traditionally inhibited by the 'no politics' rule, although at certain times the rule has been bent or circumvented. One such was the agitation leading up to the Reform Act of 1867 when the London Trades Council made a great deal of the going in the capital. George Odger saw reform as bringing an end to injustices of all kind and ending the necessity for strike action. It was he and George Howell who set up the Trade Unionists' Manhood Suffrage and Vote by Ballot Association in 1862 (101), which merged with the Reform League with its middle-class radical supporters in 1865. Even then trade union support was far from universal and Brand makes the point that the 'vast majority stood aloof'. The great exception was Birmingham where twenty unions formed branches of the League. In the national campaigns in 1866 other towns, including Manchester, Leeds, Glasgow and Edinburgh, held mass meetings in support with an impressive turnout of local leaders. In Glasgow, too, Alexander Macdonald of the miners and the Glasgow Trades Council were mounting another campaign to get the revision of the hated Master and Servant Act which Brand says was producing 10,000 prosecutions a year (101).

Political action after 1867 was carried on under the wing of the Liberal Party and through the Parliamentary Committee of the TUC, set up expressly to safeguard trade union interests in the government legislation following the Royal Commission of Inquiry in 1867. That Parliamentary Committee became the agent for setting up the Labour Representation Committee from which the Parliamentary Labour Party in turn developed, composed of MPs who had been elected under its flag. The Labour Party in the House in the period under discussion was basically a means by which trade union concerns could be more effectively aired in Parliament, a logical development from the work of the Parliamentary Committee itself, a watchdog at a different level and an ally still of the great Liberal Party. Problems implicit in having a trade union party in Parliament which might become the party in power were still far in the future but could on a grander scale throw up problems analogous to those of cooperating with employers in joint boards.

The provincial initiative in calling the TUC was of profound importance to the future of the trade union movement, principally in its early years through its action in setting up the Parliamentary Committee and through the activity of the secretary to that committee. From 1871 to 1875 this was George Howell, a Liberal and activist in the Reform League. When he resigned he was succeeded by Henry Broadhurst the leader of the Stonemasons, another Liberal; in 1890, Charles Fenwick, a Liberal MP and Northumberland miner, followed but was defeated in 1894 in the ballot for the secretaryship by another miner, Sam Woods.

The Liberal ideology of the Parliamentary Committee was most effectively displayed under Sam Woods's secretaryship in 1894. The ILP had been gaining ground among trade unions in the West Riding and among the trade councils, and had secured the passing in Congress of a resolution calling on trade unionists to support parliamentary candidates committed to collective ownership and control of production, distribution and exchange. A subcommittee of the Parliamentary Committee proposed an alteration of rules which had the effect of excluding trades councils' representatives and anyone not a worker or a union official. Under this rule both Keir Hardie and the Liberal Henry Broadhurst were excluded, and the danger of a socialist takeover of the TUC was averted.

Why did unions appear, grow, survive, decline? Are there reasons general enough to include craft societies, as well as dockers' and seamen's unions? Is it first necessary to distinguish carefully between unions according to the level of skill involved and then go on to consider the nature of the industry in which they are sited? To argue that trade societies firmly built up in industrially necessary crafts would be destined to survive in the expanding economy of Victorian England unless extirpated by law – and that for dockers and for general unions the precariousness of their work foothold in the economy militated continually against them?

A different approach would argue that unions which have the social and perhaps geographical coherence of the effective branch, say in weaving or in mining, would continue to exist even in the most adverse conditions, because collective action, formalised or not, would seem natural, given the nature of the industry. Even in general unions the evidence is that they survived when there were nuclear groups which could hold together despite external pressures.

Did the decision to set up a union depend on the fusion of social need and an organiser of genius such as Will Thorne? There has been a history of unions which were tragically shortlived. Does their survival depend on other factors such as the overall state of the trade, the attitude of employers, the technological stage of the industry? How far it is labour intensive and how heavily capitalised it is — indeed on a complex of interrelated factors. The social motivation could be found in many diverse groups; the agricultural workers of Warwickshire in the 1870s, the china clay workers of Cornwall who were captured by the Workers' Union, the gasworkers in the East End in 1889. Does this susceptibility to union organisation reflect a cogent assessment by working men that their interests can best be protected by group action, by institutionalising their economic demands? Could it be partly a wish to work within a group that the Church had at one time supplied and that the Victorian liberal ethos denied them?

The trade union provided for some workers a guarantee against a workhouse burial and for all workers a sense of identity: they were identified by the union to which they belonged. With the expansion of unions between 1910 and 1914 the potential of becoming 'honourable' men was open to more and more workers, who ceased thereby to belong to the people or the mass: they belonged to a particular branch. It offered the possibility (as Methodism had done to a different generation) of participating in democratic decision-making and of securing a diplomatic and political education which would transform some unionists to members of the governing class, like Ernie Bevin of the Dockers. The union with its splendid banners, its meetings gave a ritual significance to working-class life and, perhaps most important, offered ways in which individuals could join together to secure by joint action the advancement of their particular group. The strike gave tragic evidence of the capacity to suffer to secure improvement and of the willingness to share hardship and to battle against economic oppression. It could be seen as the field of battle, or more aptly a modern war situation in which children and women as well as men suffered from hunger, from eviction, and in which the role of hero or sometimes martyr was open to all.

If unionists had the right to withdraw their labour, to strike, did employers have the complementary right to employ 'free' labour to break the strike? The use of blackleg labour had been traditional in the nineteenth century where such labour had the necessary skill and could be readily imported from different parts of the country, from Ireland or even from abroad. Collison's National Free Labour Association set up in 1893 was an attempt to regularise the practice and to make what had previously been an *ad hoc* part of a regular business operation. The right clearly existed; but it often led to violence between those on strike and the new imported labour. Much of the unions' persuasive power and political pressure was directed to securing the right to peaceful picketing but the achievement of this right in 1875 did not guarantee the maintenance of civil peace should a strike take place. In the long term, for employers the use of free labour could be disruptive in industrial relations on the plant, and the maintenance of production by these means might sour the atmosphere on the site so much for the future that overall productivity might be impaired.

By 1914 trade union organisation had barely affected women in industry. There were several pockets in which they were strongly represented, notably in cotton, but the expansion of union membership was to wait on the changed industrial situation brought about by war and call up. Barbara Drake (45) makes the point that 'according as the men's trade unions are strong, female labour is entirely prohibited . . . or women are restricted to certain inferior branches of the industry, or to certain unorganised districts. She concludes that

the comparatively favourable working conditions enjoyed by men in organised trades have been mainly built up by their own exertions in the past, and they are not disposed to share those advantages with a new host of women competitors. Membership of trade unions was basically a male preserve, women's pay scales were far lower than those of men on equal work and membership on equal terms was to wait until the change in the status of women which was still very much in the future.

The trade union was still not the normal way of life even for the male worker in British industry, but had by 1914 come to be accepted, even assimilated, as the appropriate means by which collective bargaining should be pursued. The trade union offered far more than this to its members. No one can read the account given to the Webbs in 1893 [doc. 20] without realising what the trade union offered in political education, in social recognition, in social security and, above all, in that enhancement of personal dignity. Trade unionists were worthy men, deliberating, discussing, training themselves in democratic processes. The union provided a means of reasoned discussion, of self and group discipline, which, for working men, could be found nowhere else, except perhaps in the more hierarchical society of church or chapel. In discussing the lack of violence in the 1926 General Strike or British immunity to political extremism in the 1930s any analysis must consider the procedures and social psychology of the trade unions as they evolved in the nineteenth century.

The early history of trade unionism began with persecution by the state, harassment by the employer, with trade societies confused with conspiracies. After the improvement in the legal situation in

1824–25, there was still a long hard battle for recognition, marked by the use of lockout and the Document on the one side, and by exclusiveness and, in some industries, undue pressure to join the union on the other. If this was the heroic age of trade unionism – and outstanding leaders did emerge, Tommy Hepburn, Alexander Macdonald, George Potter, the London Junta among them – it left as many tragedies behind as heroic ages traditionally do, evictions in the mining villages, blacklisting of good men whose only crime was a commitment to a union, starvation and poverty for families where the breadwinner was on strike. The law could still be invoked in the notorious Master and Servant Act, and employers could still refuse to employ union men. Perhaps a more relevant model is of a frontier society, for Victorian capitalism, booming, expanding, bursting at its seams, was throwing up new forms of wealth and turning some artisans into entrepreneurs and employers. Workers were skirmishing for positions in the new order, with employers hostile to any loss of prerogative which might never be regained. In such a frontier society the state had little part except to arrest the occasional wrongdoer, always a workman, for infringements of factory law by employers earned only a fine.

The second period began in the 1860s with the growth of trade union pressure groups for change in the franchise and in the Master and Servant Act, and saw the victories of the legislation of 1867-75. The balance of the constitution was changed: voting power now lay with the working class. That they were so slow to realise their new power is a comment on the diversity of trade unions, their differing sectional interests and their lack of political incentive. The achievement of the vote and full legal status seemed sufficient, perhaps all that was needed now was for the Liberal Party to recruit some experienced trade unionists to speak for working-class interests in the House. The frontier had closed and they had been brought within the pale of the constitution.

The counter-attack of the employers in the 1890s, the Taff Vale decision, the socialist emphasis on the collective problems of poverty and unemployment gave a new cutting edge to trade union activity in the third phase in the years before the first World War. The state, by industrial injuries legislation, old age pensions, insurance against unemployment and sickness, began to recognise the size of the problem, but powerful groups like the dockers and the railway workers were still treated as if they belonged to that deferential society which had supported much of Victorian rural England. Conciliation and collaboration had developed in some industries but the machinery was usually very slow-moving. The bitterness and frustration is summed up in

Ben Tillett's comments [doc. 19]. They had their organisation, their political party, but the basic problems of poverty, irregularity of income and the threat of immediate dismissal remained.

Documents

The Statute of Artificers 1563

An early attempt to relate wages to the cost of living

XI. And for the declaration what wages, servants, labourers and artificers, either by the year or day or otherwise, shall receive, be it enacted, that the justices of the peace of every shire . . . within the limits of their several commissions . . . and the sheriff of that county if he conveniently may, and every mayor, bailiff or other head officer within any city . . . shall before the 10th day of June next coming, and afterward yearly at every general sessions first to be holden after Easter, or at some time convenient within six weeks next following Easter, calling unto them such discreet and grave persons of the said county or city as they shall think meet, and conferring together respecting the plenty or scarcity of the time and other circumstances necessary to be considered, have authority within the limits of their several commissions to rate and appoint the wages as well of such artificers . . . or any other labourer, servant or workman whose wages in time past hath been by any law rated and appointed, as also the wages of all other labourers, artificers (etc) which have not yet been rated, as they shall think meet to be rated (etc) by the year or by the day, week, month or other wise, with meat and drink or without meat and drink, and what wages every workman or labourer shall take by the great for mowing, reaping and threshing (and other agricultural employment) and for any other kind of reasonable labours or service, and shall yearly before the 12th July next after the said assessment made, certify the same.

A.E. Bland, P.A. Brown, and R.H. Tawney, *English Economic History*, Bell, 1914.

Industrial Workers Petition against the Repeal of the Statute of Artificers

The cotton weavers tried to secure the protection of the state against employers by petitioning the Commons against repeal in 1813. The Act was repealed in the following year.

... and that the present bill to repeal the aforesaid law has sunk the spirits of the petitioners beyond description, having no hope left; and that although the said law of 5 Eliz. was wisely designed to protect all trades and workmen, yet none will essentially suffer by its repeal save the cotton weavers; the silk weavers have law to secure their prices, as have other artisans; tradesmen generally receive their contracted wages, but cotton weavers, when their work is done, know not what they shall receive, as that depends upon the goodness of their employer's heart: And that the petitioners, therefore most humbly, and earnestly pray, that the House, for the aforesaid reasons, will not repeal the said Statute of 5 Eliz, it being the only law by which they can hope any relief from their present misery ... but should the House see it proper to repeal the said law, the petitioners pray, that in that case it will enact a law to secure and grant such wages to the petitioners as will enable them to live by their industry, equally beneficial to masters and workmen.

A. Aspinall, *Early English Trade Unions*, Batchworth Press, 1949.

document 3

The French Revolution and working classes

An extract from a letter, typical of many sent by Lancashire magistrates to the Home Office in 1791, linking the events in France with the growth of trade societies.

Thomas B. Bayley J.P. and Henry Norris, J.P. to Henry Dundas 19 July 1971, from Hope, near Manchester:

We have also now a very general spirit of combination amongst all sorts of labourers and artisans, who are in a state of disaffection to all legal control. The introduction of machinery to abridge labour in weaving, is also a subject, at this time, of peculiar disgust and jealousy. And, I fear ... an unhappy party spirit about the Revolution in France, heightened by the meetings on July 14th (which I believe none of the magistrates in this County approved, countenanced or attended) has added to the general ill-humour and may be a pretext for mischief and outrage.

Thomas B. Bayley J.P. and Henry Norris, J.P. to Henry Dundas 19 July 1791, from Hope, near Manchester: Aspinall, *ibid.*

document 4

An early general union

These extracts from the resolution passed at the first meeting of the Grand General Union of all the Operative Spinners of the United Kingdom in 1829 stress both the exclusiveness (para 18) and the respectful attitude to employers (para 27) which the union tried to foster.

18. That no person or persons be learned or allowed to spin after the 5th of April 1830 except the son, brother or orphan nephew of spinners, and the poor relations of the proprietors of the mills, and those only when they have attained the full age of 15 years. . . . Any person acting contrary to this shall be fined for the first offence in the sum of half a guinea, for the second one guinea, and for the third to be expelled from the society and have his name exposed throughout the whole trade.

19. That any person who may take work as a spinner at any rate below what is considered a fair and legal price shall be fined £5 and continue a regular paying member of all fair dues and demands for one year before he be entitled to the benefits of the trade and any member causing one under his control to do so shall be fined in one half that sum and be exposed throughout the whole trade.

24. That female spinners be urged to become members of an association to be formed exclusively for themselves, and that an entrance ceremony be prepared for them suited to their circumstances, and that they pay into and receive from their own fund such sum or sums as they may from time agree upon and they receive all the aid of the whole confederation in supporting them to obtain men's prices, or such remuneration for their labour as may be deemed sufficient under

121

general or particular circumstances.

27. That it is not the intention of this Association either directly or indirectly to interfere with, or in any way to injure the rights and property of employers or to assume or exercise any control or authority over the management of any mill or mills, but, on the contrary, will endeavour as far as in us lies to uphold the just rights and reasonable authority of every master, and compel all the members of this association to pay a due obedience and respect to their respective masters, and all their confidential servants in authority under them, our only object being to uphold the best interest of our common country by averting all the horrid train of direful calamities, which have already made too much progress amongst us and which are inseparable from cruel poverty, ignorance, degradation, pauperism and crime, and to obtain for our families the common comforts and conveniences of life.

G.D.H. Cole and A.W. Filson, *British Working Class Movements: select documents* 1789–1875, Macmillan, 1951.

document 5

The Grand National Consolidated Trades Union

The most famous attempt in early industrial England to form a general union. This document shows that in structure the GNCTU was based upon a vertical organisation of trade societies with a horizontal committee comprising the governing body.

Rules and Regulations of the Grand National Consolidated Trades Union of Great Britain and Ireland, instituted for the purpose of the more effectively enabling the working classes to receive, protect and establish the rights of industry.

GENERAL PLAN AND GOVERNMENT
I. Each trade in this Consolidated Union shall have its Grand Lodge in that Town or City most eligible for it, such Grand Lodge to be goverened internally by a Grand Master, Deputy Grand Master, and Grand Secretary, and a Committee of Management.

II. Each Grand Lodge shall have its District Lodges, in any number to be designated or named after the town or city in which the District Lodge is founded.

III. Each Grand Lodge shall be considered the head of its own particular trade, and to have certain exclusive powers accordingly; but in all other respects the Grand Lodges are to answer the same ends as the District Lodges.

IV. Each District Lodge shall embrace within itself all operatives of the same trade, living in smaller towns or villages adjacent to it, and shall be governed internally by a president, vice-president, secretary, and a committee of management.

VIII. The General government of the GNCTU, shall be vested in a Grand Council of Delegates from each of the Central Committees of all the Districts in the Consolidated Union, to be holden every six months, at such places as shall be decided upon at the preceding Council; the next meeting to be held on the first day of September, 1834, and to continue its sitting so long as may be requisite.

IX. During the recess of the Grand Council of Delegates, the government of the consolidated Union shall be vested in an Executive Council of five; which Executive will in future be chosen at the Grand Delegate Council aforesaid.

XV. No strike or turn-out for an *advance* of wages shall be made by the Members of any Lodge in the Consolidated Union without the consent of the Executive Council; but in all cases of a *reduction* of wages the Central Committee of the District shall have the power of deciding whenever a strike shall or shall not take place, and should such Central Committee be necessitated to order a levy in support of such strike brought on by such reduction of wages, such order shall be made in all the Lodges; in the first instance, in the District in which such reduction hath taken place, and on advice being forwarded to the Executive they shall consider the case, and order accordingly.

[Article XLVI in the constitution sets out the objectives of the Union, industrial and political.]

XLVI. That, although the design of the Union is, in the first instance, to raise the wages of the workmen, or prevent further reduction therein, and to diminish the hours of labour, the great and ultimate object of it must be to establish the paramount rights of Industry and Humanity, by instituting such measures as shall effectually prevent the ignorant, idle, and useless part of society from having that undue control over the fruits of our toil, which, through the agency of a vicious money system, they at present possess; and that, consequently, the Unionists should lose no opportunity of mutually encouraging and assisting each other in bringing about a DIFFERENT STATE OF THINGS, in which the really useful and intelligent part of society only shall have the direction of its affairs, and in which well-directed industry and virtue shall meet their just distinction and reward, and vicious idleness its merited contempt and destitution.

Cole and Filson, *ibid.*

document 6

The Document

The Document was the undertaking signed by workers pledging themselves not to join a trade union. This practice by employers was aimed at rooting out trade unions in their workshops and was the cause of continuing bitterness and conflict in industrial relations. Both the examples quoted here were used in the building trade, the first in 1833 and the second in 1859.

[a] We, the undersigned ... do hereby declare that we are not in any way connected with the General Union of the Building Trades and that we do not and will not contribute to the support of such members of the said union as are or may be out of work in consequence of belonging to such union.

[b] I declare that I am not now, nor will I during the continuance of my engagement with you, become a member of or support any society which directly or indirectly interferes with the arrangements of this or any other establishment or the hours or terms of labour, and that I recognise the right of Employers and Employed individually to make any trade engagements on which they may choose to agree.

Quoted in R. Postgate, *The Builders' History,* National Federation of Building Trade Operatives, 1923.

The 'New Model'

These rules of the Amalgamated Society of Engineers emphasise the industrial evils which the traditional craft societies strove to stamp out; systematic overtime, piecework and the use of workers who had not served an apprenticeship to the craft.

1 That in order to secure to our members a good general prospect of employment, we repudiate 'systematic overtime' as being the cause of much evil, through giving to a number the privilege of working more than a legitimate week's time, whilst doing so deprives other members of situations, producing much domestic misery and causing a great expenditure of the Society's funds. We, therefore, authorise the Executive Council to take steps for its immediate discontinuance by ascertaining the opinions of our members and the practices of the various localities in relation thereto, and issuing a general order for all districts simultaneously to adopt this resolution. Any member refusing to comply with this resolution renders himself liable to be excluded. The district committee shall decide upon all cases of exemption from this resolution, which shall be in cases of accident, etc, to machinery, requiring instant and continuous attention.

2 That the same steps be take to abolish piecework, to destroy the practice of working more than one lathe or machine, to prevent a greater number of apprentices or admission into one trade than are likely to find employment therein – apprentices to be in the proportion of one to four journeymen; and to endeavour by all reasonable means to assimilate the number of working hours in each district, so that uniformity may pervade the trade rules, in order that on subsequent occasions, if circumstances require a further reduction of the hours of labour, such may be accomplished without one district having to make greater advances than another.

3 If constrained to make restrictions against the admission into our trade of those who have not earned a right by probationary servitude (apprenticeship), we do so knowing that such encroachments are productive of evil and when persevered in unchecked, result in reducing the condition of the artisan to that of the unskilled labourer, and confer no permanent advantage to those admitted. It is our duty, then, to exercise that same care and watchfulness over that in which we have a vested interest, as the physician does who holds a diploma, or the author who is protected by 'copyright'.

Quoted in S. Webb and B. Webb, *Industrial Democracy* (63).

document 8

Mutual help

The practice of 'tramping' to find work was widespread in the nineteenth century and created a network of mutual help schemes amongst the craft unions. An unemployed printer or stonemason, for example, could expect to find bed, money and assistance from his fellow workers in any English town. Cheap postage, fast railways and better times in the second half of the nineteenth century slowly brought this practice to an end.

My trades union had relieving stations in nearly every town, generally situated in one of the smaller public houses. Two of the local masons are appointed to act as relieving officer and bed-inspector. The duty of the latter is to see that the beds are kept clean, in good condition, and well aired, and the accommodation is much better than might be expected. When a mason on tramp enters a town he finds his way to the relieving officer and presents his card. On this card is written the applicant's name and last permanent address. In addition, he carries a printed ticket bearing the stamp of the last lodge at which the traveller received relief. He was entitled to receive a relief allowance of one shilling for twenty miles and threepence for every additional ten miles traversed since his last receipt of relief money. Thus, if fifty miles have been covered the man receives one and ninepence. In addition, he is allowed sleeping accommodation for at least one night, and if the town where the station is situated is of considerable size he is entitled to two or three nights lodging. Besides a good bed, the proprietor of the official quarters is bound to furnish cutlery, crockery and kitchen conveniences for each traveller, that the relief money can all be spent on food. There is no temptation to spend the small sum received in intoxicating drink unless its recipient chooses to do so. The system is so perfect that it is a very rare occurrence for an impostor to succeed in cheating the union. Unfortunately the stations did not exist everywhere and where they are separated by forty or fifty miles – not a rare occurrence in the southern counties – the travellers life becomes a hard one.

Henry Broadhurst, *Story of his Life from a Stonemason's Bench to the Treasury Bench*, Hutchinson, 1901.

document 9

Trade unions and politics

After the formation of the Reform League in 1864 some prominent trade unionists helped to campaign for the extension of the franchise. George Odger, a member of the 'Junta' was particularly active and is here (in the Workman's Advocate 1865) explaining the social value of the vote for working men.

We have been asked what we shall gain by the vote when we get it. Our answer is a plain one; the working man's daughter shall not be driven into the close garret or unwholesome workshop, there to labour fourteen or sixteen hours a day, sometimes all night, for a poor and beggarly subsistence. They should go forth and see nature, they should have leisure hours to acquire those attributes which would help to make them intelligent and useful wives. Poor boys shall receive a better education and not be thrust into mines before they were strong enough for the work. The poor agricultural worker should not be compelled to work and maintain his family upon eight shillings a week, nor yet sent to gaol for taking a bit of old wood to kindle a fire to warm a sick wife.

The machine . . . should become a blessing to mankind as it was intended and not be used to drive families upon the world to live or starve as the case may be. A change in the law should not starve hundreds of ribbon weavers, nor cotton panics make the industrious workman a pauper or a dependent upon charity; these things and a great many more should be done away with. The working man with the vote would feel himself free and independent; self-reliance, that noble soul-animating quality would fully develop itself to the benefit of the whole of the community.

Quoted by C. Brand, *American Historical Review*, **30** (1924–25), 101.

document 10

The Royal Commission on Trade Unions 1867–9

The Royal Commission set up after the Sheffield Outrages gave trade unions and employees an opportunity to set out their respective cases. The 'Junta' was particularly concerned to emphasise the respectable face of trade unions at a time when there was a danger that their new standing in the industrial world might be emperilled by the violence of the sawgrinders in Sheffield.

[a] AN EMPLOYER'S VIEW
A.J. Mundella, Liberal M.P. and Nottingham employer explains to the Royal Commission the benefits of arbitration.

And you have had great experience of the representatives of the men in your part of England? — Yes. What sort of men have you found them to be? — I will tell you what has been the effects of our board of arbitration. The very men that the manufacturers dreaded were the men sent to represent the workmen at the board. We found them the most straight-forward men we could desire to have to deal with; we have often found that the power behind them has been too strong for them; they are generally the most intelligent men; and often they are put under pressure by workmen outside to do things which they know to be contrary to common sense, and they will not do them. They have been the greatest barriers we have had between the ignorant workmen and ourselves, and I know that this is so. I have found it in my correspondence with trade union secretaries and leaders; all over England I have found that so. I have known that they are opposed to most of the evils that pervade the trades unions, but there are some that are not so.

[b] STRIKES
William Allan of the Engineers explains his and his union's attitude to strikes.

Do you find that the possession of very large funds, and the fact that they belong to a very powerful organisation, such as your society is, lends generally to make the members of your society disposed to enter into such a dispute, or the contrary? 'I should say that the members generally are decidely opposed to strikes, and that the fact of our having a large accumulated fund tends to encourage that feeling amongst them. They wish to conserve what they have got . . . and we believe all strikes are a complete waste of money, not only in relation to the workmen but also to the employers.'

[c] RESTRICTIVE PRACTICES
James Clarke, of the Stockport Bricklayers' Union suggests ways in which bricklayers can bring pressure upon employers.

An 'understanding', the object of which is to support trade unions, has recently been come to between the bricklayers and the brickmasters of Stockport, to the effect that the former will not set bricks made by non-union men, and that the latter will not supply bricks to employers with whom the bricklayers have a dispute.

[d] THE MINERS'TRADE UNIONS
This is an extract from the evidence given by John Normansell of the South Yorkshire Miners' Association emphasising their twin concerns: improving legislation and friendly society benefits.

The South Yorkshire Miners' Association has many objects. First, to raise from time to time by contribution among the members funds for the purpose of mutual support. Secondly, to assist its members in striving to obtain better legislation for the efficient management of mines, whereby the health and lives of the miners may be prolonged. Thirdly, compensation for accidents when the employers are liable. Fourthly, to assist all lodges and members when unjustly dealt with by their employers or agents. Fifthly, a weekly allowance to members when injured following their employment. Seventhly, a grant of £8 at the death of any member caused by accident while following his employment. Eightly, to shorten the hours of labour, and to infuse steadier habits of working among all its members. Ninthly, to secure the true weights of the miners' material at the pit banks, thus giving to both employers and employed their legitimate due. Tenthly, to abolish all illegal stoppages at the pay offices, and to secure the prices and wages that the members may at all times bargain for. Eleventhly to improve the miners' positions, morally, mentally and physically. Twelfthly, to extend the associations' principles to our less fortunate brethren by aiding all other similar associations that have for their objects the rights of labour. Thirteenthly, a weekly allowance to the widows and orphans of members who lose their lives by accident while following their employment. These are the benefits of general association. The benefits of our local lodges are, a weekly allowance to members when sick from natural causes, an allowance of £4 at the natural death of any member, an allowance of £2 at the death of a member's wife, an allowance of £1 at the death of a member's child if under 12 years of age.

document 11

The right to combine

The Royal Commission, while admitting the right to form to trade unions, stressed the corollary right of workers to remain outside the union.

With regard to the general question of the right of workmen to combine together for determining and stipulating with their employer the terms on which only they will consent to work for him, we think that, provided the combination be perfectly voluntary, and that full liberty be left to all other workmen to undertake the work which the parties combining have refused, and that no obstruction be place in the way of an employer resorting elsewhere in search of a supply of labour, there is no ground of justice or of policy for with-holding such a right from the workmen. . . .

In every bargain there is, more or less, a struggle between the buyer and the seller, the seller desiring to get as much as he can, and the buyer to pay as little as possible; but as bet-ween the employer and the workman, there is in general this advantage on the side of the employer, that he can more easily wait – i.e., can hold out longer than the work-man. . . . It is to redress this inequality that the power of combining is justified by the promoters of trades unions.

But upon the same principle and for a precisely similar reason, we think that whilst conceding to such workmen as desire to exercise it an extended right to combine against their employers, especial care should be taken that an equal right be secured to those workmen who desire to keep aloof from the combination, to dispose of their labour with perfect freedom as they severally think fit. The power of working, and consequently the value of a man's labour varies in different individuals according to their strength, their skill, and their industry. The workmen who think it for their own advantage to combine together in the disposal of their labour are no more justified in constraining any other workman, who does not desire such association, to combine with them – to bring his labour into common stock as it were with theirs; and it is the more important that the law should protect the non-unionist workman in his right freely to dispose of his labour as he thinks best, because, standing alone he is the less able to protect himself.

Eleventh Report of the Royal Commission on Trade Unions, 1867–69.

document 12

The Railwaymen's case

[a] *This document is a copy of a petition sent in 1867 to the London and South-Western Railway management humbly asking for improve-ment in conditions of service.*

131

Gentlemen,

We, the enginemen and firemen employed by the London and South-Western Railway under you, have been long conferring together respecting our conditions, and have unanimously agreed to a series of resolutions regarding certain alterations to the terms of our engagements which we respectfully submit to your consideration, and which we conceive would be for the benefit of the company were they adopted. We are induced to put them before you as a whole because if granted in that way, it would remove all cause of dissafisfaction and stimulate the servants of the company to the active and conscientious discharge of their duties. We are desirous of asking nothing that is unreasonable, and will be glad to receive and answer any suggestions you may offer on the subject.

1. That ten hours constitute a day's work, all over ten to be paid for at the rate of two hours for a quarter. All Sunday duty to be paid for at time and a-half.

2. That 150 miles for passenger men on the main line be equal to one day's work; 120 miles for local and branch lines.

3. That a stated day be allowed in each week from 9 a.m. to 3 p.m. and if required to work on that day to be paid for at time and a-half.

4. That drivers' wages be as follows: First six months, 6s per day; second six months 6s 6d per day; after twelve months, 7s 6d per day.

5. That firemen's wages be: First six months, 3s 6d per day; second six months, 4s per day; twelve months, 4s 6d per day.

6. That every engineman and fireman being sent away on duty rendering it necessary for him to reside away from home shall be allowed for his expenses 2s 6d per night.

7. That an overcoat be supplied to every engineman and fireman once a year, and that they be allowed to retain the old one.

8. That, as a rule, all enginemen and firemen have nine hours clear off duty before being called upon to go out again.

We beg also to call your attention to the fact that £10 has been deducted from the wages of the drivers, and £5 from those of the firemen. With this arrangement we are dissatisfied, and beg most respectfully in all cases where this has been done that such amount be returned. We likewise desire to suggest that, if possible, no enginemen or firemen shall work more than every alternate Sunday.

We beg to state that many enginemen and firemen have been subject to heavy fines and punishments without having a fair or impartial hearing, and if we are not satisfied with our superintendent's decision that we should by a committee of enginemen and firemen be allowed the privilege of placing the matter before you.

G.W.Alcock, *Fifty Years of Railway Trade Unionism*, Co-operative Printing Press, 1922.

[b] *Public concern for the implications of overwork on the railways was evidenced in the setting up of a Royal Commission on Railway Accidents (1877). This is an extract of the evidence given to the Commission by Weston, driver on the North British.*

... I have been on duty 16 hours in succession, and on the third day I went on the engine at 7.30 in the morning and left it as a rule at 11 or 12 at night if we were in to our time. I ran for 250 miles. In that time I was never allowed to leave the engine. I took my meals and everything on the engine. It was a passenger engine. I never left the engine. I complained to my fireman and told him that I found difficulty in keeping my eyes open. Upon the third day I said to him that I could not hold myself responsible if anything occurred to the engine or passengers., and that it was unfair to force us to do it. He reported this to the superintendent, Mr Wheatley. He called me up, and said: 'Weston, unless you retract those words I will dismiss you! I said: 'Mr Wheatley, you have the power to dismiss me, but I cannot retract what I said.' I was compelled to do it, but I told him honestly that in coming home, running for 250 miles, when I came in at night I found myself falling asleep.

Quoted by N. McKillop, *The Lighted Flame* (14).

The dockers' call-on

The call-on was the degrading practice by which dockers had to stand at the ready hoping to be picked out for work by the foreman, a practice especially humiliating to men as independent as dockers.

At that time the 'call-ons' took place frequently in the day, and they seemed to be calculated to inflict upon the dock workers the maximum of inconvenience, discomfort, anxiety, and misery. The first call of the day was at seven o'clock in the morning. A second took place just before eight o'clock, a third forty-five minutes later, and a fourth at a quarter to one. In the interval of calls the unfortunate wage-slaves who had not caught the foreman's eye had to loaf about and kill time as best they could. In wet and cold weather their misery can better be imagined than described.

Ben Tillett, *Memories and Reflections* (4).

The dockers' strike, 1889

The dockers' strike, which drew massive trade union support, particularly from Australia, and attracted great public sympathy, was the culmination of long-standing grievances over pay and conditions of work. The following is the first manifesto issued by the Joint Strike Committee.

To the Trade Unionists and other workmen of the United Kingdom. Fellow working men: the dock labourers of London, the poorest, most wretched and worst paid men in London are on strike for an advance of a penny an hour day work and twopence per hour overtime. The amount of work, these men may obtain, is only on an average three or four hours a day; with this they have to suffer under a system of sub-contract which permits them to be driven like slaves, at the bidding of men who are selected from the most brutal of their class, who underpay, overdrive and restrict the numbers necessary to do a fair day's work. Knowing this we, the whole of the dock workers of London, stevedores, painters, scalers, corn porters, steel porters, coal heavers, ballast heavers, wharf labourers, shoe gangs, dockmen, seamen and firemen, carmen, lightermen, barge men, steering hands, hydraulic crane drivers, tugmen, etc., etc., have ceased work to support these poor men. We are also calling on all the other trades of London to support us, and will surely win if we receive that support. We therefore appeal with confidence to all Trade Unions, especially those whose work is in connection with shipping. We also appeal to the public at large for contributions and support on behalf of the dock labourers. . . . In doing so we feel sure that our effort will be appreciated, not as disturbers or peace-breakers, but as a demand from men determined to swerve not one inch from the attitude they have taken up to succour the poor, and lift up the downtrodden.

Quoted in Tillett, *ibid.*

document 15

The miners' strike, 1893

Although conciliation and arbitration procedures were well established in many industries, including mining, what was unprecedented in the mining strike of 1893 was the intervention of the Prime Minister, an implicit acceptance of the position of government as an interested party to disputes which could seriously damage the nation's economy.

10 Downing Street
November 13 1893

Sir, The attention of Her Majesty's Government has been seriously called to the widespread and disastrous effects produced by the long continuance of the unfortunate dispute in the coal trade which has now entered its sixteenth week.

It is clear from the information which has reached the Board of Trade, that much misery and suffering are caused not only to the families of the men directly involved, but also to many thousands of others, not engaged in mining, whose employment has been adversely affected by the stoppage. The further prolongation of the dispute cannot fail to aggravate the suffering, especially in view of the approach of winter, when the greatly increased price of fuel is likely to cause distress among the poorer classes throughout the country.

The Government have not, up to the present, considered that they could advantageously intervene in a dispute, the settlement of which would far more usefully be brought about by the action of those concerned in it, than by the good offices of others. But having regard to the serious state of affairs referred to above, to the national importance of a speedy termination of the dispute, and to the fact that the Conference which took place on the 3rd and 4th November did not result in a settlement, Her Majesty's Government have felt it their duty to make an effort to bring about a resumption of negotiation between the employers and the employed, under conditions which they hope may lead to a satisfactory result.

It appears to them that advantage might accrue from a further discussion between the parties of the present position of matters under the chairmanship of a member of the Government who it is hoped will not be unacceptable to either side.

Lord Rosebery has consented, at the request of his colleagues to undertake the important duty which such position involves.

I have therefore to invite the Miners' Federation to send representatives to a conference to be held forthwith under his chairmanship.

In discharging this duty it is not proposed that Lord Rosebery should assume the position of an Arbitrator or umpire, or himself vote in the proceedings, but that he should confine his action to offering his good offices in order to assist the parties in arriving between themselves at a friendly settlement of the questions in dispute.

I am,
Your obedient and faithful servant,
W.E. GLADSTONE

T. Ashton Esq.,
General Secretary,
Miners' Federation of Great Britain.

Quoted in R. Page Arnot, *The Miners* (16) vol 1.

The origins of the Labour Party

In 1899 the TUC finally accepted the view of the socialists that working-class interests would best be served by the creation of an independent party in the House. This resolution passed by the TUC in that year calls for the setting up of a joint committee to bring this about, the committee which came to be called the Labour Representation Committee. Powerful unions like the miners and the textile workers were strongly opposed even to this rather half-hearted move towards independent representation.

That this Congress having regard to its decisions in former years, and with a view to securing a better representation of the interests of Labour in the House of Commons hereby instructs the Parliamentary Committee to invite the co-operation on lines mutually agreed upon in convening a Special Congress of representatives from such of the above named organisations as may be willing to take part to devise ways and means for securing the return of an increased number of Labour members to the next Parliament.

Quoted in Henry Pelling, *The Origins of the Labour Party 1880-1900* **(54)**.

Syndicalism

Syndicalists rejected the cooperation with the capitalist state which collective bargaining procedures and the existence of a Labour Party working within the constitution clearly implied. They emphasised the ultimate goal of the new society which could be achieved by 'direct action'. In their view each strike had to be seen as a means of achieving a society based upon workers' control and the final seizure of power would crown a general strike. In France, in Catalonia, in Ireland as well as in the United States syndicalism in varying forms and with varying success had taken root. The Miners' Next Step, published by the South Wales Miners Federation in 1912, stands as the clearest British statement of syndicalist ideas formed in the context of militant mining unionism in the Welsh coalfields.

The policy of conciliation gives the real power of the men into the hands of a few leaders. . . . In the main and on things that matter, the Executive have the supreme power. The workmen for a time look up to these men and when things are going well they idolise them. The employers respect them. Why? Because they have the men – the real power – in the hollow of their hands. They, the leaders become 'gentlemen, they become M.P.'s and have considerable social prestige because of this power. Now when any man or men assume power of this description, we have a right to ask them to be infallible. That is the penalty, a just one too, of autocracy. When things go wrong, and we have shown that they have gone wrong, they deserve to be, and are blamed. What really is blameworthy, is the conciliation policy which demands leaders of this description. . . .

Ultimate objective
One organisation to cover the whole of the Coal, Ore, Slate, Stone, Clay, Salt, mining and quarrying industry of Great Britain, with one Central Executive.

Programme-political
That the organisation shall engage in political action both local and national, on the basis of complete independence of, and hostility to all capitalist parties, with an avowed policy of wresting whatever advantage it can for the working class.

General
Alliances to be formed, and trades organisations fostered, with a view to steps being taken, to amalgamate all workers into one National and International union, to work for the taking over of all industries, by the workmen themselves. . . .

It will noticed that nothing is said about Conciliation Boards or Wages Agreements. . . . Conciliation Boards and Wages Agreements only lead us into a morass. . . . the suggested organisation is constructed to fight rather than to negotiate. It is based upon the principle that we can only get what we are strong enough to win and retain.

Quoted in W.H.B. Court, *British Economic History 1870–1914*, Cambridge University Press, 1965.

The Army and the Welsh miners

[a] *General Sir Nevil Macready, who wrote this account, was sent by Winston Churchill as Home Secretary to South Wales in 1910 to command troops to back up the police during a strike involving the use of blackleg labour. What is perhaps most remarkable is his heavily jocular manner in describing the use of bayonets against the strikers.*

. . . The golden rule that the soldiers were not to come into play until the police had exhausted all their resources was rigorously adhered to, and owing to the large numbers of police who had been drafted into the district the military rarely came into contact with the mob. In the Tonypandy Valley, however, the rioters found that the police with their heavy greatcoats and somewhat robust physique were handicapped when following agile young stone throwers up the steep tracks that ascend the hill-side at right angles to the main road in the valley.

During the rioting that occurred on 21st November throughout the Tonpandy Valley the Metropolitan Police while driving the mob before them along the main road were heavily stoned from the side tracks, and suffered severe casualties. In order to counter these tactics on the part of the strikers on the next occasion when trouble was afoot, small bodies of infantry on the higher ground, keeping level with the police on the main road, moved slowly down the side tracks, and by a little gentle persuasion with the bayonet drove the stone-throwers into the arms of the police on the lower road. The effect was excellent; no casualties were reported, though it was rumoured that many young men of the valley found that sitting down was accompanied with a certain amount of discomfort for several days. As a general instruction the soldiers had been warned that if obliged to use their bayonets they should only be applied to that portion of the body traditionally held by trainers of youth to be reserved for punishment.

Quoted in R Frow, E. Frow and M. Katanka, *Strikes*, Charles Knight, 1971.

Keir Hardie's moving account of the death of the innocent in an incident in a mining strike in Llanelly in 1911.

As showing how the troops were likely to be used to shoot men down like dogs, take what happened at Llanelly. A train was stopped by a crowd of strikers squatting down on the line in front of it. Some troops, quartered at the station, rushed up at the double, and lined up on both sides of the engine. Before they got there, however, a striker had boarded the footbridge of the engine and drawn the fire, and so the engine was effectively disabled from proceeding. But for the presence of the soldiers nothing more would have happened. Some boys and youths did pelt stones at the soldiers, and one of them was struck. Mr Lloyd George spoke of what happened as being undoubtedly a 'very great riot', and described the engine driver as lying bleeding and helpless from the violence of the mob. This, however, was all imagination without an atom of truth. The train was standing in a deep cutting, and the official story is that stones were coming in showers from both sides. Now, not one pane of glass in the carriage windows was broken, not one passenger was hurt or molested, in fact, they were looking out of the windows, no civilian was struck, no property was damaged; there was no riot. But the officer in command ordered the people to disperse; he gave them one minute in which to do so; at the end of the minute he ordered five shots to be fired which killed two men outright, and wounded four others. John Johns, one of the murdered men, was sitting on the garden wall of his own house in shirt and trousers, looking on; the other was also in his garden at the top of the railway embankment. No one has ever alleged that either of them threw stones or took any part in what little stone throwing there was. Presumably, however, they made good targets, and so were picked off. For the troops are not to fire at random. They are not to use blank cartridge, even by way of warning, they are not to fire at the legs of the crowd; their instructions were to make every shot tell, they were to shoot to kill.

Frow, and Frow and Katanka (*ibid*).

A contemporary analysis of the industrial scene in 1912

Ben Tillett, the dockers' leader reports to his union. The tone is typical of the bitterness of the years before the First World War, with employers backed by army and police suppressing workers and (in Tillett's view) both Parliament and the Labour Party unwilling in one case, and unable in the other, to help.

The sequence of events in 1912 followed the usual course: claims for increases and recognition followed by refusal and consequent strikes; efforts of mediation, negotiations, conciliation; Board of Trade effort, police intimidation, coercion, brutality, riot, imprisonment; Home Secretary intervenes with armed forces, attempts at suppression, Cossack methods of Home Office forces, Parliament dumb and acquiescent, Labour Party impotent where not indifferent, struggle and end of same, in some cases with industrial gains.

The class war is the most brutal of wars and the most pitiless. The lesson is that, in future strikes, the striker must protect against the use of arms, with arms; protest against shooting, with shooting; protest against violence, with violence. . . . The other lesson is that Parliament is a farce and a sham, the rich man's Duma, the employer's Tammany, the Thieves' Kitchen, and the working man's despot. . . . In the 1912 strikes we had to fight Parliament, the forces of the Crown, the judges of the law. . . . We had the press of both parties and the capitalists against us; the police were incensed by the employers and rewarded for every act of violence, the imported police as usual being the worst of the brutes. . . . Capitalism is capitalism as a tiger is a tiger; and both are savage and pitiless towards the weak.

Quoted in Alan Bullock, *The Life and Times of Ernest Bevin* (8), vol. 1.

Trade unionism as a social educator

[a] *The oath taken by Thames Watermen at a ceremony held in the Hall of the Watermen's Company, St Mary-at-Hill, London and described by Harry Gosling in his autobiography.*

... to learn his Art, and with him (after the manner of an Apprentice) to dwell and serve upon the river of Thames from the Day of the Date hereof until the full End and Term of seven years from thence next following, to be fully complete and ended; during which Term the said Apprentice his said Master faithfully shall, serve as aforesaid, his Secrets keep, his lawful Commandments everywhere gladly do; He shall do no damage to his said Master nor see it to be done by others, but that he to his power shall let or forthwith give Warning to the said Master of the same; He shall not waste the Goods of the said Master, nor lend them unlawfully to any; He shall not commit Fornication, nor contract Matrimony within the said Term; He shall not play at Cards, Dice, Tables nor any other unlawful games whereby his said Master may have any loss. With his own Goods or others during the said Term, without License of his said Master he shall not buy nor sell; He shall not haunt Taverns nor Play Houses, nor absent himself from his Master's service Day nor Night, unlawfully, but in all things as a faithful Apprentice he shall behave himself towards his said Master and all his during the said Term.

Harry Gosling, *Up and Down Stream* (12).

[b] *This description of trade union proceedings was given to the Webbs by a skilled craftsman in 1893. It underlines the fundamental value of the unions in teaching democratic organisations and in schooling the British working class in techniques of disciplined and constitutional procedures.*

He is now an ordinary member of the Lodge and this newly acquired dignity is fully brought home to him in the course of a week or so, when he receives his first summons to attend a Lodge meeting. The men come in by twos and threes, and he notices that, with few exceptions, all are neat and clean, having been home and had their tea and a wash in the interval between then and working hours. Shortly after the hour fixed for commencing the President takes the chair, and, as the men slowly straggle into the room, rises and declares the meeting open for business. The clubroom is a long, low ceiling room which constitutes the first floor of the public house. . . . Down the centre of the room runs a trestle table with forms along the sides, on which members are seating themselves. At the top a shorter table is placed crosswise, forming a letter T, and here sits the group of officers.

The first business of the evening is the payment of contributions. The Secretary, aided by the 'Check Secretary', the Money Steward, and Treasurer, receives the subscriptions from the men as they come, one by one, up the room, enters the payment in the books, and signs the members cards. When the subscriptions are all received, the unemployed members, and the wives or other relatives of those who are sick, present themselves to draw their respective benefits. General inquiries are made after the health and hopes are expressed for the speedy recovery of the sick ones; and the sums due are paid out by the officials with considerable formality. . . .

The President rises and calls for order. Strangers and non-members are cleared out of the room. The doorkeeper takes up his position inside the door to watch the comers-in and goers-out; and the drink stewards make ready to attend to the members' wants and act as waiters, in order to dispense with strangers in the room, and to prevent any unnecessary bustle and confusion. The business of the meeting opens with the reading of the minutes of the last meeting . . . the minutes are confirmed by a show of hands and signed by the President. .·. .

The Lodge meeting soon plays an important part in the life of our active-minded artisan. He feels that he is taking part in the actual government of a national institution.

Quoted in S. Webb, and B. Webb, *History of Trade Unionism* (25).

Bibliography

PRIMARY SOURCES

Reports of:

Select Committee on Artisans and Machinery, 1824.
Select Committee on the Combination Laws 1825.
Select Committee on Combinations of Workmen 1837–38.
Royal Commission on Trade Unions 1867–69.
Select Committees on the Settlement of Disputes between Masters and Operatives, 1856–60.
Select Committee on the Contracts of Service between Master and Servant, 1865-6.
(All the above documents have been reprinted by the Irish University Press in its series *Industrial Relations*.)
Royal Commission on Labour, 1891-94.

National Association for the Promotion of Social Science, *Trade Unions and Strikes*, 1860.

BIBLIOGRAPHIES

Frow, R., Frow, E. and Katanka, M. *The History of British Trade Unionism; a select bibliography*, Historical Association pamphlet H76,1969.
Society for the Study of Labour History, *Bulletin*.

COLLECTIONS OF DOCUMENTS

Cole, G.D.H. and Filson, A.W. *British Working Class Movements: Select Documents, 1789–1875.*
Aspinall, A. *Early English Trade Unions*, Batchworth Press, 1949.
Frow, E. and Katanka, M., eds. *1868, Year of the Unions,* Michael Katanka, 1968.
Frow, R., Frow, E. and Katanka, M., *Strikes*, Charles Knight, 1971.

145

BIOGRAPHIES

1 Saville, John and Bellamy, Joyce M., eds. *Dictionary of Labour Biography*, 4 vols, Macmillan, 1972–77.
2 Thale, Mary, ed. *The Autobiography of Francis Place*, Cambridge University Press.
3 Radice, Giles and Radice, Lisanne. *Will Thorne, Constructive Militant*, Allen & Unwin, 1974.
4 Tillett, Ben. *Memories and Reflections*, John Long, 1931.
5 Larkin, Emmet. *James Larkin, Irish Labour Leader 1876–1947*, Routledge & Kegan Paul, 1965.
6 Mann, Tom. *Memoirs* Macgibbon & Kee, 1967.
7 Torr, Dona. *Tom Mann and his Times* Lawrence & Wishart, 1956, vol 1.
8 Bullock, Alan. *The Life and Times of Ernest Bevin*, Heinemann 1960, vol 1.
9 Horn, Pamela. *Joseph Arch*, Kineton, 1971.
10 Ashby, M.K. *Joseph Ashby of Tysoe*, Cambridge University Press, 1961.
11 Leventhal. F.M. *Respectable Radical: George Howell and Victorian working-class politics*, Weidenfeld & Nicolson, 1971.
12 Gosling, Harry. *Up and Down Stream*, Macmillan, 1927.
13 Broadhurst, Henry. *The Story of his Life from a Stonemason's Bench to the Treasury Bench*, Hutchinson, 1901.

HISTORIES OF INDIVIDUAL TRADE UNIONS

14 McKillop, Norman. *The Lighted Flame*, Nelson, 1950.
15 Evans, E.W. *The Miners of South Wales*, University of Wales Press, 1961.
16 Arnot, R. Page. *The Miners 1889–1945*, 3 vols, Allen & Unwin, 1949–61.
17 Groves, Reg. *Sharpen the Sickle*, Porcupine Press, 1949.
18 Postgate, R. *The Builders History*, National Federation of Building Trades Operatives, 1923.
19 Turner, H.A. *Trade Union Growth, Structure and Policy*, Allen & Unwin, 1962 (for textile workers).
20 Jefferys, J.B. *The Story of the Engineers*, Lawrence & Wishart, 1945.
21 Lovell, J. *Stevedores and Dockers*, Macmillan, 1969.
22 Musson, A.E. *Typographical Association*, Oxford University Press, 1954.
23 Alcock, G.W. *Fifty Years of Railway Trade Unionism*, Co-operative

Printing Press, 1922.

24 Bagwell, P.S. *The Railwaymen*, Allen & Unwin, 1963.

GENERAL

25 Webb, S. and Webb, B. *History of Trade Unions*, Longmans, rev. edn, 1920.
26 Hammond, J.L. and Hammond, B. *The Town Labourer*, Longmans, 1949.
27 Musson A.E. *Trade Union and Social History*, Frank Cass, 1974.
28 Thompson, E.P. *The Making of the English Working Class*, Penguin (Pelican) 1963.
29 Pelling, H. *History of British Trade Unionism*, Macmillan, 1963.
30 Cole, G.D.H. *Attempts at a General Union 1818–1834*, Macmillan, 1953.
31 Lewis, Brian. *British Coal Mining in the Eighteenth and Nineteenth Centuries*, Longman (Seminar Studies In History), 1971.
32 Pollard, S. *A History of Labour in Sheffield*, Liverpool University Press, 1969.
33 Corbett, J. *The Birmingham Trades Council 1866–1966* Lawrence & Wishart, 1966.
34 Roberts, B.C. *The Trades Union Congress 1866–1921*, Allen & Unwin, 1958.
35 Musson. A.E. *The Congress of 1868*, TUC, 1935.
36 Clegg, H.A. Fox, A. and Thompson, A.F. *A History of British Trade Unions since 1889*, Oxford University Press, 1964 vol 1.
37 Fraser, W.H. *Trade Unions and Society:the struggle for acceptance 1850–1880* Allen & Unwin, 1974.
38 Saul, S.B. *The Myth of the Great Depression 1873–1896*, Macmillan, 1969.
39 Rowntree, B.S. *Poverty: a study of town life*, John Long, 1899.
40 Checkland, S.G. *The Upas Tree: Glasgow 1875–1975*, University of Glasgow Press, 1976.
41 Harrison, Royden. *Before the Socialists*, Routledge, 1965.
42 Pelling, H. *Popular Politics and Society*, Macmillan, 1968.
43 Clarke, P.F. *Lancashire and the New Liberalism*, Cambridge University Press, 1971.
44 Briggs, Asa. *Chartist Studies*, Macmillan, 1959.
45 Drake, B. *Women in Trade Unions*, Allen & Unwin, 1921.
46 Hoggart, Richard. *The Uses of Literacy*, Chatto & Windus, 1957.
47 Hyman, R. *The Workers Union* Oxford University Press, 1972.
48 MacDougall, I. *The Minutes of the Edinburgh Trades Council 1859–73*, Constable, 1968.

49 Flinn, M.W. and Smout, T.C. *Essays in Social History*, Oxford University Press, 1974.

50 Flanders, A.F. *Trade Unions*, Hutchinson, 1968.

51 Cole, G.D.H. *A Short History of the British Working Class Movement* Allen & Unwin, 1948.

52 Trades Union Congress, *The Martyrs of Tolpuddle*, 1934.

53 Dangerfield, George. *The Strange Death of Liberal England* Macgibbon & Kee, 1966.

54 Pelling, H. *The origins of the Labour Party 1880–1900*, Oxford University Press, 1965.

55 Bowley, A.L. *Wages and Income in the United Kingdom since 1860*, Oxford University Press, 1937.

56 Tsuzuki, C. *H.M. Hyndman and British Socialism*, Oxford University Press, 1961.

57 Phelps Brown E.H. *The Growth of British Industrial Relations*, Macmillan, 1959.

58 Bagwell, P.S. *Industrial Relations*, Irish University Press, 1974.

59 Lovell, John. *British Trade Unions 1875–1933*, Macmillan, 1977.

60 Charles, Rodger. *The Development of Industrial Relations in Britain 1911–39*, Hutchinson 1973.

61 Clegg, H.A. *The System of Industrial Relations in Great Britain*, Blackwell, 1972.

62 Collins, Henry and Abramsky, C. *Karl Marx and the British Labour Movement*, Macmillan, 1965.

63 Webb, S. and Webb, B. *Industrial Democracy*, Longmans, 1920.

64 Bealey, F. and Pelling, H. *Labour and Politics*, Macmillan, 1958.

65 Gregory, Roy. *The Miners and British Politics*, Oxford University Press, 1968.

66 Gwyn, William B. *Democracy and the Cost of Politics in Britain*, Athlone Press, 1962.

67 Askwith, Lord *Problems and Disputes*, The Harvester Press, 1974.

68 Brown, Kenneth D. *Labour and Unemployment 1900–1914*, David & Charles, 1971.

69 Hinton, James. *The First Shop Stewards' Movement*, Allen & Unwin, 1973.

70 Webb, Beatrice. *Our Partnership*, Longman, 1948.

71 Musson, A.E. *British Trade Unions 1800–75*, Macmillan, 1972.

72 Allen, V.L. *The Sociology of Industrial Relations*, Longman, 1971.

73 Harrison, J.F.C. *The Early Victorians 1832–52* Weidenfeld & Nicolson, 1971.

74 Musson, A.E. 'The Webbs and their phasing of trade union development between the 1830s and the 1860s', *Labour History Society*

Bulletin, no. 4 (Spring 1962).

75 Tate, G. *The London Trades Council 1860–1950* Lawrence & Wishart 1950.

76 Thompson, E.P. *The Making of the English Working Class*, Penguin (Pelican), 1963.

77 Browne, Harry *Joseph Chamberlain, Radical and Imperialist*, Longman (Seminar Studies in History), 1974.

ARTICLES

78 George, M.D. 'The Combination Laws reconsidered', *Economic History* (supplement to *Economic Journal*), 2 (May 1927) and 'The Combination Laws', *Economic History Rev.* 6 (1936).

79 Oliver, W.H. 'The consolidated trades of '34, *Economic History Rev.* 2 ser., 18 (1964).

80 Allen, V.L. 'A methodological criticism of the Webbs as trade union historians', *Labour History Bulletin*, no. 4 (Spring 1962).

81 Cole, G.D.H. 'British trade unions in the third quarter of the nineteenth century', in E.M. Carus-Wilson, ed. *Essays in Economic History*, vol. 3.

82 Burgess K. 'Technological change and the 1852 lock-out in the British engineering industry', *International Review of Social History* 14 (1969).

83 Taylor, A.J. 'The Miners' Association of Great Britain and Ireland', *Economica* 22 (1955).

84 Saville, John 'Trades Councils and the Labour Movement to 1900', *Labour History Society Bulletin*, 14 (Spring 1967).

85 Dunbabin, J.P.D. 'The Revolt of the Field: The Agricultural Labourers' Movement in the 1870s', *Past and Present*, no 26, 1963.

86 Peacock, A.J. 'The Revolt of the Field in East Anglia', in L.M. Munby, ed. *The Luddites and Other Essays*, Michael Katanka, 1971.

87 Bagwell, P.S. 'The Triple Industrial Alliance 1913–22', in A. Briggs, and J. Saville, eds, *Essays in Labour History 1886–1923*, Macmillan, 1971.

88 Phillips, G.A. 'The Triple Industrial Alliance in 1914', *Economic History Rev.*, 2nd ser 24, 1, (1971).

89 Coltham, Stephen. 'The Beehive Newspaper: its origins and early struggles', in Briggs and Saville, *op. cit.*

90 Clements, R.V. 'Trade unionism and emigration', *Population Studies* 9 (1955).

149

91 Saville, John 'Trade unions and free labour: the background to the Taff Vale decision' in Briggs, and Saville, *op. cit.*

92 Erickson, C 'The encouragement of emigration by British trade unions 1850–1900', *Population Studies* 3 (1949–50).

93 Shepperson, W.S. 'Industrial emigration in early Victorian Britain', *Journal of Economic History*, 13 (1953).

94 Porter, J.H. 'Wage bargaining under conciliation agreements 1914', *Economic History Rev.*, 2nd ser., 23 (1970).

95 Clements, R.V. 'British trade unions and popular political economy 1850–75', *Economic History Rev*, 2nd ser., 14 (1961).

96 McCormick, B and Williams, J.E. 'The miners and the eight-hour day 1863–1910', *Economic History Rev*, 2nd ser., 12 (1959).

97 Neale, R.S. 'Class and class consciousness in early nineteenth century England', *Victorian Studies* 12 (1968).

98 Prothero, I 'Chartism in London' *Past and Present*, 44 (1969).

99 Prothero, I. 'London Chartism and the Trades', *Economic History Rev.*, 2nd ser., 24 (1971).

100 Rowe, D.J. 'The failure of London Chartism' *Historical Journal* 11 (1968).

101 Brand, C.E. 'The conversion of the British trade unions to political action', *American Historical Review*, 30 (1925).

102 Hicks, J.R. 'The early history of industrial conciliation in England', *Economica*, 10 (1930).

103 Odber, A.J. 'The origins of industrial peace: the manufactured iron trade of the North of England', *Oxford Economic Papers*, new ser. no. 3, (1951).

104 Brunner, E. 'The origins of industrial peace: the case of the British boot and shoe industry', *Oxford Economic Papers*, no. 2 June 1949.

105 Taylor, A.J. 'Labour productivity and technological innovation in the British coal industry 1850–1914', *Economic History Rev.*, 2nd ser. 14 (1961-2).

106 Allen V.L. 'The Origins of Industrial Conciliation and Arbitration' *International Review of Social History*, 9 (1964).

107 Hobsbawm, E.J. 'The machine breakers', in *Labouring Men*, Weidenfeld & Nicolson, 1964.

108 Hobsbawm, E.J. 'The tramping artisan', in *ibid*.

109 Hobsbawm, E.J. 'The labour aristocracy', in *ibid*.

110 McCready, H.W. 'British Labour and the Royal Commission on Trade Unions' *University of Toronto Quarterly*, 24 (1955).

111 McCready, H.W. 'British labour's lobby 1867–75', *Canadian Journal of Economics and Political Science*, 22 (1956).

112 Briggs, Asa, 'Robert Applegarth and the Trade Unions' in *Victorian People*, Penguin (Pelican) 1965.

113 Gupta, P.S. 'Railway trade unionism in Britain, 1880–1900' *Economic History Rev.*, 2nd ser. **19** (1966).

114 Sires, R.V. 'Labour unrest in England', *Journal of Economic History*, **15** 1955).

115 Crossick, G. 'The labour aristocracy and its values', *Victorian Studies* 1976.

116 Hobsbawm, E.J. 'British gasworkers 1973–1914', in *Labouring Men*, 1964.

Index

153